THE AWAKENED LIFE FOR HIGH SCHOOL STUDENTS

FINDING STILLNESS IN AN ANXIOUS WORLD

LEADER GUIDE

Sarah E. Bollinger

Angela R. Olsen

UPPER ROOM BOOKS®
NASHVILLE

CONTENTS

WELCOME

Wake up! This is not your typical Bible study. This is an invitation to awaken to life. Too many of us are overwhelmed by anxiety, depression, worry, loneliness, and fear. Stressed and distracted, we miss so much of what makes life wonderful. We believe there is an alternative.

Within these pages, faith, practice, and science come together. We share the science behind the ways mindfulness and spiritual practices can reduce anxiety, worry, and depression. We explore practices of prayerful meditation that allow us to calm our minds, to slow down amid the pressures of life, and to find stillness in an anxious world. In this stillness, we can be present to the grace and love of God—and there, we can find wholeness and joy.

> [Jesus said,] "I came that they may have life, and have it abundantly."
> JOHN 10:10

Daily spiritual practices open us to the abundant life God offers each of us. An abundant life is not one free of pain and worry but rather one rich in the beauty of all life has to offer—sadness *and* joy, seriousness *and* celebration, the ordinary *and* the transformational. Over the course of the next eight weeks, we invite you and your high school students to explore new ways to get the most out of each moment and to see what God is doing in you, in your relationships, and in the world around you. We hope the practices you adopt and the insights you gain about yourself each week will bring you closer to God, help you build strength to face life's struggles, and awaken you to the joy of a more abundant life.

Your sisters,

Sarah & Angie

GETTING STARTED

The Awakened Life for High School Students is designed for youth workers and church leaders who work with high school students. Our hope is that this small-group study provides tools and practices that will help you empower students to live a more abundant life.

WHAT THIS STUDY IS AND WHAT IT IS NOT

We take seriously the alarming research showing that depression, anxiety, suicide, and other mental health issues are on the rise among young people. Many church leaders and youth workers admit that the declining emotional, mental, and spiritual health among high school students is an ever-increasing area of concern in their ministry; yet, they rarely feel equipped to help students cope with these issues. *The Awakened Life for High School Students* offers a way to address these concerns. This eight-week study is designed to help church leaders and youth workers guide high school students through practices that build resiliency, develop psychosocial skills, and foster emotional and spiritual well-being.

This is not a traditional Bible study. While we use scripture and talk about well-being from a United Methodist theological perspective, this is not simply a scriptural study of well-being. In the same vein, this is not a clinical intervention. We do not intend for this to be a replacement for mental health treatment or therapy. Referral to necessary mental health resources is the correct response to a mental health crisis or symptoms that could lead to a diagnosis of mental illness.

This is a resource to equip those in nonclinical roles who are working on the front lines with students; it is designed for those who provide spiritual and emotional care to students but who are not counselors or therapists. Furthermore, this resource leans on the idea that our faith can help us to assist students in building resiliency and developing psychosocial skills. It was conceptualized to respond to nonclinical issues of well-being among students with an intentional focus on using our faith tradition and practices to inform this work.

Mindfulness and Christianity

Christianity and mindfulness go hand in hand. One way we address student well-being in this study is through using both spiritual practices and mindfulness techniques. Research shows that mindfulness practices, including meditation, contribute to improved mood, increased concentration, and healthier relationships. Our faith tradition also has a lot to add to the conversation around mindfulness, and we share rich contemplative practices that point to this truth. With this knowledge in mind, we approach this study with the intention of empowering students to be more present and able to navigate emotional disturbance. (For those who are interested in reading more about the connection between Christianity and mindfulness, Amy G. Oden's book *Right Here, Right Now* is a wonderful resource.[1])

HOW THIS GUIDE WORKS

This study walks through eight weeks of practices and reflections. Each weekly session is about an hour long and includes a spiritual practice that you can explore as a group. In each session, prayer and meditation techniques are coupled with discussion, activities, and journaling. Plan to give your students sufficient space and time to work through the content.

You can tailor the sessions to suit the students in your group. Each week contains one key practice that is central to the week's big idea; it can be a guidepost for how you choose to lead each session. The weekly plans include information, discussion questions, activities, and instructions for facilitation. If you don't make it through every activity or discussion, that is perfectly all right. Videos, audio tracks, and other ancillary resources are available at UpperRoomBooks.com/TheAwakenedLife. The website also offers supplemental content—additional exercises for optional use as well as devotionals written by and for teens that relate to each session.

The content for this study is organized into three central components: connection to self and the work of the divine within, connection to others in meaningful relationship, and connection to creation. The sessions begin with an introductory week, then follow this flow: two weeks understanding our relationship with ourselves, two weeks deepening our relationships with others, two weeks connecting with nature, and, finally, a closing session in week eight. Here is a brief outline of the study:

Week 1. Introduction to the Awakened Life

Week 2. Connection to Self: Noticing Thoughts

Week 3. Connection to Self: Being Present in the Body

Week 4. Connecting to Others: Working Through Loneliness

Week 5. Connection to Others: Working Through Shame

Week 6. Connecting to Creation: Experiencing Awe of Nature

Week 7. Connecting to Creation: Sharing a Meal of Intention

Week 8. Closing: Awakening to Joy

Weekly Content

Each week's session will follow the same rhythm by revisiting the following five elements:

 Awake: Sessions will begin with an **introductory section** on waking up to the abundant life God offers each of us. This section is the students' call to wake up, join in, and participate in this work each week. It is inspired by a moment in Jesus' life when he was seeking connection and support from his friends in moments of struggle. Three times he found them asleep in the garden of Gethsemane and unable to join with him in prayer during his most critical moment of need. (See Matthew 26:36-46.) How often are we asleep to what God is doing in our midst?

 Aware: From awakening we will move into a greater awareness of what can hold us back from abundant life. This section will contain **scientific studies and real-life examples** that illustrate what living a disconnected life does to the body, mind, and spirit. Naming our distractions, conflicts, and anxieties will begin to remove their power over our lives. This section is inspired by our desire not to be conformed to this anxious world. (See Romans 12:1-2.) We will become aware of how our minds are being transformed and opened to experience God's perfect goodness and wholeness.

Alive: Becoming alive involves engagement. This section contains **journal prompts and group exercises** to help students embody and bring to life the topics at hand. This section is inspired by the Creation story, when God breathes life into humanity. (See Genesis 2:7.)

Abide: This section offers **spiritual practices** handed down through the generations and intended here to connect students with God at work in themselves, in their relationships, and in the world. This section was inspired by Jesus' invitation to remain in his love. (See John 15:5-11.) Each practice is a means of experiencing this divine, unconditional love. These grace-filled practices help us to abide deeply in God's love, and they help restore the image of God in us all.

Arise: This section offers a **summary** of the session and reviews the assignments to be completed between sessions. Students are asked to practice daily and to write about their experience so that they can go out into the world equipped and energized to engage in new ways. This section was inspired by the resurrection of Jesus Christ, and this incredible power of bringing life out of death is available to us as well. (See John 11:25-26.) Students can carry this hope with them during this group study and beyond.

Establishing Boundaries and Building Trust in a Closed Group

The content in this study is best suited for a small group—ideally, ten to fifteen high school juniors and seniors. Please be aware that this study works best when used with a "closed group" in which participants attend consistently and the same group members attend each week. Be sure the students you invite to participate are aware of this expectation before they commit to join the group. Regular attendance allows for lasting change among group members.

You will want to establish boundaries and guidelines to set the stage for the work that you will do together during these eight sessions. This study assumes that you will be working with a previously established group of young people who are familiar with you and with one another. However, we recognize that you may be inviting a new group of students or a subset of your usual youth group to participate in this study. Especially if students are new to one another, we encourage you to work as a group to create a covenant that will serve as agreed-upon guidelines for your time together. (An exercise for "Making a Covenant" can be found online at UpperRoomBooks.com/TheAwakenedLife.) You may want to gather the students once before the study begins to create your covenant, review the "Getting Started" section of the Student Guide, and get to know one another.

Practicing at Home

Each week will include a mindfulness or spiritual practice—a short, manageable exercise for students to practice daily between sessions. The Student Guide outlines these practices and provides space for students to write or draw about their experiences each day. The journaling exercises they do in each session will model ways they can record their daily observations between sessions. In each session, you can introduce the practice, try it once with the students, and allow them some time to record their first entry in their practice journal. There is not a right or wrong way to do the home practices; the important thing is that the students begin and keep at it. As the group leader, it is important for you to model this habit and establish your own rhythm of practice as well.

Assigning Practice Partners for Accountability

We highly recommend that students be asked to encourage and hold one another accountable for completing the daily practice and any other weekly assignments. Assigning practice partners who check in on each other from week to week increases individual accountability and group cohesiveness. You might want to decide on these practice partner assignments before the first session. We suggest pairing students who are similar in age and who are not in a dating relationship. If you think this material will be challenging for your students, you might pair teens who are already comfortable together. Pay attention to the way partner relationships develop over the eight weeks. If you find that a pair is not getting along, you will want to address the problem before it becomes a distraction.

How to Talk About Difficult Topics

As you invite students to talk, write, or draw about difficult topics, you may encounter periods of silence. Silence can indicate a need for reflection before speaking or writing. You can let your students know in advance that silence is OK; it can be a welcomed guest in the process.

Certain topics that you will discuss might be difficult for some students or might elicit strong memories and reactions. As you facilitate these conversations, you may want to adopt a "trauma-informed care" approach.[2] Be sensitive to students' personal histories; keep in mind that some students may have faced painful experiences in the past that caused psychological harm. Try to ensure that all students feel safe—both physically and emotionally. Invite them to participate in what they feel comfortable doing. If students choose not to engage in a discussion or activity, that is OK. Welcome them to join; don't force them.

You are not expected to be a mental health expert. If issues arise, you can—and should—refer students to a pastor or professional counselor. These signs may indicate that a student requires clinical assistance: difficulty controlling emotional response, excessive worry or fear, avoidance of friends or activities, self-harming behavior, or extreme mood changes. If you need help discerning when to refer a student for additional care, these websites offer helpful resources: https://www.nami.org/Learn-More or https://www.mentalhealthfirstaid.org/mental-health-resources/.

A Note About Learning Styles

This study offers multiple ways for students to engage with the material. Sessions include group discussions and partner conversations as well as time for individual reflection. Journal prompts can be used to inspire written or drawn responses. Other activities range from group research to movement exercises. Pay attention to the preferences of students in your group. When possible, set up the sessions in a way that allows students to choose how they would like to engage. For instance, during times of personal reflection, you might make available a range of materials (pens, colored pencils, markers, and lined and unlined paper) and allow students to stretch and move as needed. Then, students can choose if they wish to reflect by writing, drawing, or even pacing around the room.

Things to Plan For

For each week, the Leader Guide features a materials list, schedule overview, and leader preparation notes, which include details about any special requirements for each session. As the leader of this group, you will benefit from reading these notes and reviewing the session plan before your group meets. While the sessions do not require extensive preparation, here are some logistics to be aware of as you plan the weekly content.

- You may want to set up the room in a way that is conducive to "heart and soul work." Consider scents, sounds, sights, textures, and movements that would foster a safe, peaceful, and contemplative atmosphere.

- Week 5 invites students to participate in a love feast. The session outline includes the liturgy and instructions for the service. You will want to invite students to help you plan and lead this celebration.

- Week 6 involves a prayer walk. You may want to arrange for your group to meet at a nature preserve or park. If you are unable to leave your church grounds, you will want to consider the best location for this walk or to prepare a PowerPoint of nature scenes.

- Week 7 involves preparing and sharing a meal together. Make necessary arrangements as you see fit. You can ask students to bring ingredients for a meal you will make together, coordinate a potluck, or place an order for delivery. If you will be making a meal, you may want to find produce that is locally grown.

- Week 8 suggests giving each student a token of course completion as an symbol of your time together. If you choose to do this, you will want to preorder or prepare anything that you might need. If you decide to give a picture of the group as your token, make sure to take this photo a few weeks in advance and print copies.

Student Guide

The Leader Guide has been developed to be used in tandem with the Student Guide. The Student Guide provides instructions for group activities and daily practices as well as space to write or draw in response to journal prompts related to each week's theme. Because of the personal nature of many of the journal prompts, you will want to provide one Student Guide per student and ensure that privacy is maintained. The Student Guide was created for students to use during the session (for following along with the session content) and throughout the week (for reviewing the practice instructions, keeping a practice log, and writing or drawing in the journal space).

The Leader Guide incorporates text from the Student Guide for your convenience. When you, as the leader, are prompted to read this material aloud or to explain it to the group, the relevant page number in the Student Guide will be included so that you can invite students to follow along. Still, it may be useful to you to review the Student Guide before you distribute copies to your students so that you know what they will see each week.

If purchasing copies of the Student Guide is not an option for your group, you may want to provide small composition books or ask students to bring their own journals so that they can respond to the prompts. You also will want to have pens, pencils, paper, and other drawing materials available each week in case students forget to bring their journals.

Doing Your Own Work

We are firm believers in the idea that you can learn with and from your students. One of the most challenging aspects of this curriculum is that it requires you, as the leader, to model and practice mindfulness and well-being alongside your students. This means that you will need to be actively engaged in your own "heart and soul work." You will want to take part in the daily practices, and you may even want to use a Student Guide or journal to respond to prompts along with your students.

Remember that skill-building and self-awareness take time. Regular practice is encouraged to bring about lasting change. Here are some tips we offer to ensure consistency:

- **Set an alarm** for the same time every day to remind you to practice.
- **Keep a journal**. Reflect on your practice as part of your daily routine.

- **Extend compassion to yourself.** Everyone feels a little awkward when they start these practices, but your life will be better if you put in the effort.

This study also provides opportunities for you to share from your own experience. Speaking from a place of depth is critical in these moments. We encourage you to share the ways you have awakened to your own life.

BLESSINGS ON THE JOURNEY

We hope this study offers a way for you and your group to find stillness in an anxious world, to be present to God's love and grace, and to discover the wholeness, hope, and joy that God's love and grace provide. We encourage you, as the leader on this journey, to be curious, open, and present to a process that can bring about great transformation. May you be filled with grace, and may you model what it means to live the awakened life in a world full of sleepers.

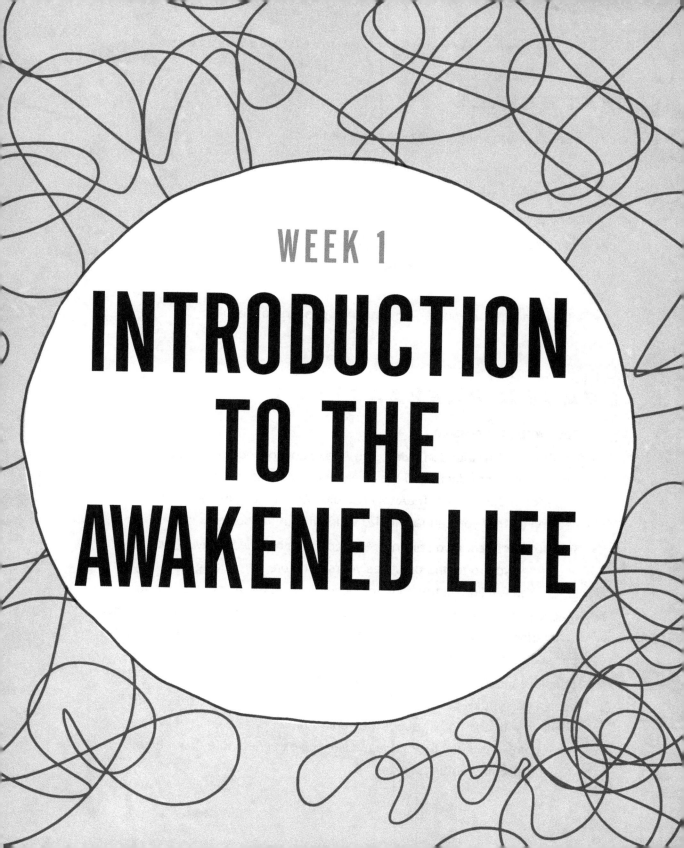

WEEK 1

INTRODUCTION TO THE AWAKENED LIFE

MATERIALS

For this session, you will need the following items:

- Large self-adhesive easel paper
- Small sticky notes
- Markers
- Pens and pencils
- Student Guides and/or journals
- Bibles
- Internet access, computer, screen, and speakers (optional)

LEADER PREPARATION

- **Review the full session**.
- **Preview the introduction video**. The Awake section incorporates a video called "Introduction to the Awakened Life." It is available at UpperRoomBooks.com/TheAwakenedLife. Watch the video before the session so that you can familiarize yourself with the content.
- **Try the practices.** If you are new to meditation or to *lectio divina,* we encourage you to try the practices yourself before introducing them to your group. You will find instructions for *lectio divina* in the Abide section. To practice the meditation, use the audio track for Week 1 (*"Week 1: Awareness Meditation"* available at UpperRoomBooks.com/TheAwakenedLife) or read the audio script in the Aware section.
- **Consider practice partner assignments**. We recommend that you assign each student a practice partner. Between sessions, partners will check in with each other about their daily home practices and help each other complete these tasks. Please see the extended note about these assignments in "Getting Started."

- **Procure, review, and distribute Student Guides**. The Student Guide includes instructions for group activities and the home practices. It also provides journal space for writing or drawing as well as prompts related to each week's theme. For your convenience, the Leader Guide will provide page numbers for these relevant materials in the Student Guide. You might want to flip through the Student Guide in advance of each session so that you know what content students will see. This week, you may want to give each group member a Student Guide and spend a little time pointing out any features you think might be especially helpful for your group.

SCHEDULE FOR WEEK 1

A schedule will be provided for each session. The schedule is intended to give you an overview of what to expect in the session. These schedules also are posted online at UpperRoomBooks.com/TheAwakenedLife so that you can display them for your group. Students often appreciate knowing what will happen during the session; this added element of structure can decrease the anxiety that can arise in new situations.

 AWAKE (10–15 MINUTES)
    CHECK-IN
    INTRODUCTION
    GROUP ACTIVITY

 AWARE (10–15 MINUTES)
    THE WHY
    INTRO TO MEDITATION

 ALIVE (10–15 MINUTES)
    JOURNAL

ABIDE (10–15 MINUTES)
LECTIO DIVINA

ARISE (5–10 MINUTES)
REVIEW HOME PRACTICES
CLOSING BLESSING

AWAKE (10-15 MINUTES)

The opening section of Week 1 invites students to begin a journey of awakening to abundant life. If you have gathered a new group of students for these sessions, be aware that they will be getting to know one another for the first time. If the group has been meeting for a while, you may want to explain what will make this study unique during this introductory session.

CHECK-IN

Begin with an opening ritual. Your youth group may already have one. If not, you might try saying a short prayer together or lighting a candle to symbolize Christ's presence.

Then, invite the students to respond to the question that follows with one word or a short phrase. Students can answer in "popcorn style," chiming in with their answers when they feel comfortable. Encourage students to participate, but do not require them to speak.

- *How do you wake up in the morning (alarm, snooze, no snooze, music, etc.)?*

INTRODUCTION TO THE AWAKENED LIFE

To introduce students to the big idea, you may want to read aloud the following paragraph. (These paragraphs are also located on page 12 of the Student Guide.)

> *Even after you get out of bed in the morning, do you ever feel as if you sleepwalk through your day? Do your thoughts wander so much that you miss what is happening right in front of you? For the next eight weeks,*

we will be practicing ways to fully wake up to our lives. The biblical term abundant life can help us understand what it means to be awake and fully alive. Abundance describes a state of being connected, healthy, and whole. Unfortunately, many of us miss out on this awakened and abundant life. We focus on negative things that happened in the past, we are distracted by our screens, or we worry about things that might happen in the future. We miss the fullness and joy that are at our fingertips. Abundant life does not mean life without struggle or pain but rather a life deeply connected to what God is doing in the moment—in us, in our relationships with others, and in the world around us. When living an abundant life, hope and joy are accessible, even in the midst of struggle.

You may want to share your own story about waking up to God's presence as a concrete example for students. Then, explain how this study will differ from your typical group gatherings before moving deeper into the material. Be sure to establish boundaries and guidelines to set the stage for the work that you will do together during these eight sessions. In particular, we recommend that you discuss the importance of confidentiality, commitment, and consistency as you create a safe space to be vulnerable and real with one another. (For more help with this, especially if you are convening a new group of students, see "Establishing Boundaries and Building Trust in a Closed Group" on page 10 in Getting Started.)

Watch > *Introduction to the Awakened Life*

To foster a deeper understanding of what students will be doing for the next eight weeks, you may wish to play a video that introduces the big idea of the study. The video "Introduction to the Awakened Life" can be found at UpperRoomBooks.com/TheAwakenedLife.

GROUP ACTIVITY: WORD WALL

Next, give students time to gather in pairs for some conversation. Encourage them to listen closely to each other as they respond to this prompt.

- *Describe a moment in your life when you felt fully present and awake to something wonderful that was happening.*

While the students are responding, you can distribute to each student a marker and a small sticky note. Write "Awakened Life" on a giant sheet of self-adhesive easel paper; display it on a wall, a white board, a table, or another space in the room where you will be able to access it each week.

When the students have completed the listening exercise, ask each of them to write on a sticky note a word or phrase that best captures what they heard from their partner. Invite students to place the sticky notes around the words "Awakened Life" to create a word wall. Then, read aloud all the sticky notes. Let students know that during each session you will learn practices that will help you to become more and more awake to the presence of God and to the gift of abundant life.

Save the word wall so that you can add new insights to it during each session. You might use a different color sticky note for each week. The word wall can provide evidence of change and growth throughout the program.

AWARE (10–15 MINUTES)

In this section, you will explain some research about mental health and strategies for change and then invite the group to sample a brief meditation exercise.

THE WHY

To begin, you can read aloud the information that follows. (The information can also be found in the Student Guide on page 13.)

> Did you know that one in five teens live with a mental illness?[1] High school can be stressful; students can feel pressure to make good grades, to get into college or decide what to do after graduation, and to meet the expectations of parents, teachers, and friends.[2] Many teens also struggle with depression, anxiety, and other mental health issues. Anxiety and

depression may be part of your life as well. If so, hear this clearly: You are not alone. You do not have to feel ashamed. There is hope.

Fortunately, a number of strategies are available to help us build strength and resiliency. Resiliency describes our ability to "bounce back" after a difficult or traumatic experience. Mindfulness, spiritual practices, healthy relationships, and time in nature have all been scientifically proven to improve mental health. During our time together, we will explore a number of mindfulness and spiritual practices. These practices invite us to take one moment at a time and to fully live in the present. We will build an awakened life together through these simple, life-giving practices.

A NOTE ABOUT MENTAL HEALTH: This study is not intended to replace medicine and counseling, which are important and effective tools for treating mental illness. Encourage students who may be struggling with anxiety or depression to seek help. Let them know you will support them.

INTRO TO MEDITATION

Especially if meditation will be new for some of your students, you may wish to introduce the practice to them this week. Before beginning the exercise, ask students to discuss this question:

- *What experiences have you had with meditation and spiritual practices?*

After the discussion, invite students to try a short meditation exercise. The exercise will introduce them to the kind of mindfulness practices they will explore through this study—practices intended to improve mental health. Be aware that for those who are practicing meditation for the first time, this exercise might be extremely difficult. It might even be difficult for you as the leader. You are invited to share with your students your experience of learning this practice. What was it like for you when you first tried this meditation exercise? Remind students to be patient with themselves. Let them know that it's OK if this is challenging. You may want to paraphrase or read aloud the following paragraph. (It can also be found in the Student Guide on page 14.)

Awakening to God's working in and through you in the present moment takes practice. During meditation exercises, you will take time to pause and be present, to listen to your breathing, and to notice, without judgment, what is going on in your mind and body. If meditative prayer and mindfulness are not already part of your daily life, it might be difficult for you, initially, to sit in silence; and that's OK. Be kind to yourself as you learn and grow in this practice.

Listen > *Week 1: Awareness Meditation*

Transition the group into the meditation exercise. You may choose to read aloud the following script or to use the audio track online at UpperRoomBooks.com/TheAwakenedLife. If you use the script, be sure to read slowly and with intention; give students space to pause and to notice their breath and thoughts.

Take a moment to find a comfortable, upright position. Sit with your back straight, and gently rest both feet on the ground, legs uncrossed. Or, if you prefer, sit cross-legged on the floor. Rest your hands comfortably on your knees or in your lap. If you feel comfortable doing so, close your eyes. If not, simply rest your gaze on one unmoving spot a few feet in front of you.

Begin to notice your breath. Notice the ins and outs of each breathing cycle. Without judgment, notice the quality of your breath. Is it shallow? Or heavy? Is it raspy? Or short? Without trying to change anything about your breath, take a couple of moments to notice it.

As you sit breathing, you may notice that your mind begins to wander. That's OK. Without judging yourself, simply take account of when you begin to get lost in thought and gently bring your mind back to your breath.

Take a minute to practice being aware of your breath.

Together as a group, let's all take one deep inhalation and an open-mouthed exhalation. Then, slowly open your eyes when you are ready.

Prayer

As the exercise ends, ask students to say this prayer with you. (It is located on page 14 of the Student Guide.)

God, help me to be fully present and thankful for each breath. Amen.

Reflection

After the meditation exercise, encourage students to discuss this experience.

- *How did you feel while practicing this meditation?*
- *What are your initial reactions to this practice?*

Before you continue, let students know that over the course of the eight weeks they will explore both mindful meditation and Christian spiritual practices. During each session, they will be introduced to at least one new practice and invited to continue the practice at home each day between the sessions. This week, they will experience both this short meditation and a Christian spiritual practice (*lectio divina*). They will be encouraged to continue practicing *lectio divina* every day. Next week, they will deepen their experience of meditation.

ALIVE (10-15 MINUTES)

Now, you can transition the group into a time of personal reflection followed by group discussion. The journal prompts in this section ask students to explore personal experiences of wholeness or to consider what obstacles can prevent them from feeling whole. You may use the prompts in a way that best fits your group and the allotted time.

JOURNAL

You can use the paragraph that follows to explain the reflection process and to invite students to respond to the prompts in writing or drawing. Ask students to choose one or two prompts to answer. Also, consider giving students a set amount of time—five or ten minutes; a time constraint often helps students feel more comfortable with free writing or drawing.

When we use the journal prompts, today and throughout this study, feel free to respond with whatever comes to mind. You can write or draw without judgment. Don't worry about editing or erasing. Just allow yourself time to brainstorm without filtering your thoughts.

Here are the prompts the students will find on pages 15–16 of the Student Guide:

- Describe a time when you felt peaceful, connected, and whole in mind, body, and spirit. What contributed to your feeling this way?

- What pressures, demands, or expectations make your life stressful? What keeps you from feeling peaceful, connected, and whole?

- Describe a particularly difficult or stressful situation you have faced this year. How did you respond to that situation?

- When you are faced with challenges, what gives you resiliency? What helps you to "bounce back"?

- When have you felt closest to God? How did that experience affect you?

Discussion

Invite the students to share their responses with the group or with a partner. Let students know they can use what they wrote or drew as a guide and share as much or as little as they want. As you conclude the discussion, encourage students to respond to more of these prompts during the week.

ABIDE (10-15 MINUTES) ♡

LECTIO DIVINA

In this section, you will help students explore the spiritual practice of *lectio divina*.

Instructions

The instructions for practicing *lectio divina* are printed in the Student Guide on pages 17–18. Start by walking the students through these instructions using the text that follows. Let them know that they will follow these instructions when they are practicing on their own.

> *This week's spiritual practice is an ancient Christian practice called* lectio divina, *which means "divine reading."* Lectio divina *includes focused reading, meditation, and prayer. This practice begins with a prayer inviting the Holy Spirit to reveal something to you through the experience.*
>
> *When you practice* lectio divina *at home this week, you will begin by finding a quiet place to spend time with God. Then, you will choose a scripture or poem from the list on page 17 of your Student Guide. You might wish to use the same scripture or poem each day to deepen your understanding and experience of the text, but you also can use a different text each day.*
>
> - *John 10:10*
>
> - *Psalm 46:10*
>
> - *Psalm 139:13-14*
>
> - *Matthew 11:28*
>
> - *Excerpt from Hafiz, "Awake Awhile":*
>   *Awake, my dear.*
>   *Be kind to your sleeping heart.*
>   *Take it out into the vast fields of Light*
>   *And let it breathe.[3]*

- *Excerpt from John O'Donohue, "The Question Holds the Lantern":*

    Once you start to awaken, no one can ever claim you again for the old patterns. . . . You want your God to be wild and to call you to where your destiny awaits.[4]

Once you have chosen your text, find a comfortable position. Then, ask God to focus your thoughts and to reveal to you something you need to hear as you practice lectio divina. *Then, read through the selected scripture or poem excerpt three times. The first time, read it slowly in your mind. The second time, read it slowly out loud. The third time, read it again in your mind, noting which word or words stand out to you. Then, spend some quiet time listening for God's still small voice, noting further what the passage says to you. Pay attention to the way God invites you to care for your physical, emotional, mental, and spiritual health.*

Pause to ask if the students have questions about *lectio divina*. Then, guide them through this ancient prayer practice using John 10:10 (NRSV) as your text. Let students know that the group practice will be a little different from their individual practice.

Group Practice

To guide them through the practice, you can read the paragraphs that follow. Be sure to pause for a minute after each reading to allow time for students to reflect.

Today, we are going to practice lectio divina *as a group. Our group practice will be a little different from the way you will practice alone at home this week, but it will give you a good introduction to* lectio divina. *We will be focusing on the words of John 10:10. You may continue to use this verse at home this week, or you may choose another option.*

To begin, find a comfortable position. Close your eyes, if you wish, and begin to pay attention to your breathing. Ask God to help you let go of all distractions so that you might hear what God wants to say to you.

Now, listen as I read John 10:10, and pay attention to the word or phrase that stands out to you: "I came that they may have life, and have it abundantly." . . . Now, hear this verse a second time, and notice any image that comes to mind: "I came that they may have life, and have it abundantly." . . . As I read this verse a third time, listen for God's invitation to you: "I came that they may have life, and have it abundantly." . . . Continue in silence, listening for God's still small voice and noting anything else this verse might be saying to you. Pay attention to the way God invites you to care for your physical, emotional, mental, and spiritual health.

When you are ready, open your eyes.

Once your group has practiced *lectio divina*, take a moment to reflect on the practice. Now is a good time to show students the practice journal they will find in the Student Guide. (The journal pages for Week 1 begin on page 20 of the Student Guide.) Encourage students to log an entry in this journal each time they try a practice. Here's what the students will see for Day One:

DAY 1

Date: Practice:

What do you notice about your thoughts, emotions, and physical body?

Invite students to log their first entry under "Day 1" as you walk them through the process. Ask them to fill in today's date and to write "*lectio divina*" as the practice. Then, explain that you would like for them to note any thoughts or feelings that came up during the practice. Encourage students to recall what they were aware of in their bodies—tense shoulders, a knot in the stomach, restlessness, relaxed breathing, or a sense of calm. Invite them to jot down some words or doodle some pictures to capture these observations. Let students know that the purpose of the practice journal is to increase their awareness; there is no wrong answer.

Once the students have written an entry for Day 1, invite them to talk with one another about what came to mind as they practiced *lectio divina* (a word, an image, an invitation) or as they wrote in the practice journal. Then, allow them to ask you any questions they have about the practice or the journal process.

Challenge students to practice *lectio divina* each day for the next week (following the instructions on pages 17–18 of the Student Guide) and to journal each time they complete the practice.

ARISE (5-10 MINUTES)

Having a closing ritual for each session will be important. Each week, you may want to restate the session's main idea and to preview the next. Also, take time to reinforce the daily practice assignment. In addition, this week you will want to assign practice partners.

To begin, read aloud or paraphrase the paragraph that follows. (It is also found in the Student Guide on page 18.) Then walk students through their practice partner assignments and home practices before you say together the closing blessing.

> *Today you learned about the importance of being awake, aware, and alive in the moment. Next week, you will dig into the incredibly and uniquely beautiful person God has created you to be. Before the group meets again, it's important to practice regularly what you have learned so far. To notice lasting change, regular practice is key.*

PRACTICE PARTNERS

Explain that each student will have a partner who can offer support between sessions. These partners will be the same throughout the eight weeks. Partners will check in with each other about their weekly practices and help each other complete these tasks.

After you make the practice partner assignments, point students to page 18 of the Student Guide. It provides space for the student to write down his or her partner's name and contact information. Allow time for students to exchange this information before you continue.

HOME PRACTICES FOR WEEK 1

Practicing at home and keeping a practice journal will be critical components of each week. Show students where they can find the home practices for this week on page 19 of the Student Guide. Encourage students to do the following:

1. Try the Abide spiritual practice (*lectio divina*) every day. You might want to try practicing at the same time each day.

2. Keep track of your reactions and insights in the practice journal section of the Student Guide (beginning on page 20). For example, on Day 1, enter the date you practiced and the practice: "*lectio divina*." Then, record what you notice about your thoughts, emotions, and physical body. Keep in mind that there is no wrong answer.

3. Check in with your partner at least twice this week. If you want to try practicing *lectio divina* together, you can take turns reading aloud the scripture or quote you choose.

In addition to these items, you may want to ask students to read the "Welcome" (page 7) and "Getting Started" (pages 9–10) sections of the Student Guide and to jot down any questions they have about *The Awakened Life*. Reading these sections will help students to know what to expect in the weeks to come.

CLOSING BLESSING

Together, read the closing blessing, which will be the same each week. (The blessing is printed in the Student Guide on page 19.)

We are awakening to abundant life.
We are becoming aware of our worth and belonging.
We are coming alive to our senses, thoughts, and emotions.
We are abiding in the love and grace of God.
We arise now to live a life as connected, whole people.

WEEK 2

CONNECTING TO SELF

NOTICING THOUGHTS

MATERIALS

For this session, you will need the following items:

- Small sticky notes
- Markers
- Internet access, computer, and speakers (optional)
- Student Guides and/or journals
- Pens and pencils

LEADER PREPARATION

- **Review the full session**.
- **Locate the "Awakened Life" word wall.** If you started creating an "Awakened Life" word wall during the last session, make sure the students can access it again this week. If you are building it on a large sheet of self-adhesive easel paper, find a safe spot to store it between sessions. If you are using a wall or white board, you may want to find a way to ensure that the word wall will remain undisturbed for the next six weeks.
- **Try the practice.** The Awake and Abide sections include a meditation practice ("Awareness Meditation"). We encourage you to try it yourself before presenting it to your students. You can use the audio track "Week 2: Awareness Meditation" found online at UpperRoomBooks.com/ TheAwakenedLife.
- **Do your homework.** The Alive section offers an opportunity to talk with students about self-compassion. Dr. Kristin Neff, a psychologist who has researched and written extensively on the topic, says self-compassion has three elements:[1]

  1. Self-kindness rather than self-judgment

2. Mindfulness rather than over-identification with our thoughts

3. Recognizing our common humanity rather than isolating ourselves

Before talking with your students about self-compassion, you may want to explore more of Neff's work at https://self-compassion.org/the-three-elements-of-self-compassion-2/.

SCHEDULE FOR WEEK 2

 AWAKE (10–15 MINUTES)
  CHECK-IN
  INTRODUCTION
  AWARENESS MEDITATION

 AWARE (10–15 MINUTES)
  THE WHY

 ALIVE (10–15 MINUTES)
  JOURNAL
  ABOUT SELF-COMPASSION

 ABIDE (10–15 MINUTES)
  AWARENESS MEDITATION WITH COMPASSION

 ARISE (5–10 MINUTES)
  REVIEW HOME PRACTICES
  CLOSING BLESSING

AWAKE (10–15 MINUTES)

In Week 2, you will help the students begin to explore well-being from the inside out. This week's session focuses on our minds and how the practice of quieting our thoughts can help us tune in to what God is doing within us. This opening section asks students to consider their relationship with their thoughts.

CHECK-IN

Begin by lighting a candle or saying an introductory prayer. If you asked students to read the "Getting Started" section of the Student Guide as one of the home practices for Week 1, invite them to talk about what they read and to ask any questions they have about *The Awakened Life*. If not, you can begin this session by reviewing some of the important things that the group discussed during the last session. Then, using the prompts that follow, find out what the students observed as they practiced *lectio divina* during the week.

- *How did your home practice go? Which verse(s) did you use for* lectio divina? *What did you discover through reading, meditation, and prayer?*

    Invite students to review the journal entries they made between sessions. Ask them to select one or two sentences that they would like to read aloud.

- *How did your practice partner encourage you this week?*

    Take this moment to reinforce the importance of the practice partners.

- *Share a moment during the week when you felt most awake to your life.*

    Pass out small sticky notes. You may wish to provide sticky notes in a different color than the one you used in the first session. Then, invite each student to write on a sticky note a word or phrase that best captures this awake moment. Then, ask students to place the sticky notes on the "Awakened Life" word wall you began creating last week. Encourage students to look at the new experiences that have been added to the word wall. Allow time for students to ask for more information from one another about intriguing words or phrases.

INTRODUCTION TO WEEK 2: NOTICING THOUGHTS

As you introduce students to the content for this session, let them know that each week you will continue to pursue an awakened life. This week's session will focus on the mind and how noticing our thoughts and learning to monitor them can help us tune in to God's presence in our lives. You may read or paraphrase the following paragraph. (This information is also in the Student Guide on page 24.)

> *How cool is the mind—it keeps us alive! Our minds do everything from signaling our breathing to processing the words we are reading. We are designed to have our minds wander, to scan the horizon for danger, and to learn new things. It's OK for our minds to be busy, but sometimes our busy minds can get the best of us. Instead of making us more aware of our surroundings, our anxious and negative thoughts can spiral and take us completely out of the moment. The truth is that we are more than our thoughts. Thoughts can be helpful, but ultimately our thoughts change from day to day, or even from moment to moment. When we think about past regrets or worry about the future, we miss the present moment—the only moment in which we truly can be alive. Yet, we can train our minds in the same way that we train the muscles in our bodies. With training, we can notice our thoughts without allowing them to rob us of our present-moment awareness. With training, we can find amazing freedom to focus on what is truly important to us.*

Encourage the students to reflect by asking these questions:

- *What demands compete for your attention?*
- *When have your worries distracted you and kept you from paying attention to what was happening around you?*

AWARENESS MEDITATION

This week's meditation builds on the short meditation exercise the students tried last week. To introduce the awareness meditation, you may read the paragraph that follows.

As we did last week, we are going to take some time to train our minds to focus on the still small voice of God. Last week, our daily spiritual practice was lectio divina. *This week, we will practice an awareness meditation. We are going to try it together now, and we will practice it again at the end of our time together. Then, you will be invited to practice this awareness meditation on your own during the week. This meditation is an opportunity to notice our thoughts without judgment and to hear the voice of God above the noise of the world.*

Listen > *Week 2: Awareness Meditation*

Guide the students through this short meditation. You may choose to read aloud the following script or to use the audio track ("Week 2: Awareness Meditation") online at UpperRoomBooks.com/TheAwakenedLife. If you use the script, be sure to read slowly and with intention; give students space to pause and to notice their breath and thoughts.

Begin by finding a relaxed but upright position. Sit with your back straight and resting against a chair, or sit cross-legged on the floor. Rest your hands comfortably on your knees or in your lap. Close your eyes, and begin to focus on your breath.

Begin to notice your breath. Notice the ins and outs of each breathing cycle. Without judgment, notice the quality of your breath. Is it shallow? Or heavy? Is it raspy? Or short? Without trying to change anything about your breathing, take a couple of moments to be attentive to it.

As you bring awareness to your breath, allow your mind to relax. When you notice that your mind begins to wander and thoughts take you away from the present moment, gently, without judgment, bring your mind back to your breath. As you notice thoughts come and go, you can think of your thoughts as clouds in a big, blue, open sky. As thoughts come, notice that just as clouds float through the sky, your thoughts float through your mind, leaving a clear, blue sky behind. Try not to attach too much attention to each thought cloud; allow thoughts to come and go gently, coming back to an awareness of your breath whenever you need to. Take a moment to practice being aware of your breathing. As you are ready, slowly open your eyes and bring your attention back to the room.

Prayer

As the meditation ends, ask students to say this prayer with you. (It is located on page 24 of the Student Guide.)

> **God, help me to notice my own thoughts and to be thankful for my mind. Amen.**

Reflection

After the awareness meditation, ask each student to find a partner and to discuss the experience. Invite the partners to respond to these questions:

- *What thoughts did you notice during the meditation?*
- *What were your reactions to those thoughts?*

AWARE (10–15 MINUTES)

In this section, you will explore with your students the various negative thought patterns that can demand our attention.

THE WHY

Start by reading aloud the paragraphs that follow. (This information can be found also in the Student Guide on page 25.)

> *Being aware of our thoughts is important to our mental, physical, and spiritual health. Most people's minds wander; in fact, we spend almost half of our waking hours thinking about something other than what we are doing.[2] When our minds wander, we are no longer in the present moment. This habit can make us feel disconnected and unhappy.*

Thoughts can be distracting and overwhelming; but ultimately, thoughts are just thoughts. They are real but not always true. In other words, thoughts are not always facts. Thoughts come and go. Noticing and naming thought patterns, specifically the negative thought patterns that grab hold of our minds, is key to minimizing their power over our lives.

Negative Thought Patterns

Next, review some common negative thought patterns.[3] (The list of negative thought patterns that follows is also printed in the Student Guide on page 25.)

- **Catastrophizing**—jumping to the worst-case scenario
- **Mind-Reading**—assuming what others are thinking, without knowing their real thoughts
- **The "Shoulds"**—feeling as if you need to do something because of some unwritten rule
- **Blaming**—holding others responsible for your own pain and suffering
- **The Comparison Trap**—measuring yourself against your peers (often on social media)
- **FOMO (Fear of Missing Out)**—wanting to be constantly connected to what is happening

As you describe each negative thought pattern, consider providing students with an example of how that pattern manifests in real life. For instance, as you describe "blaming," you might say, "When Jack is sent to detention, he blames his teachers. He believes he is in detention because his teachers don't like him." Or when you describe "catastrophizing," you might say, "As Ava prepares for her history test, she thinks, *This will be a hard test, and I might fail it—actually, I know I will fail it! This will probably make me fail the whole class! And then I will never graduate high school or go to college!*"

Group Activity

The following scenario illustrates some of the negative thought patterns you have discussed with your students. (The scenario is also printed in the Student Guide on pages

25–26.) First, ask your students to read it once silently. Then, you might invite students to listen for the negative thought patterns at work as you read the scenario aloud.

> *Lauren was walking to class yesterday and saw her friend Rachel down the hall. They hadn't seen each other in several days, and Lauren was excited to connect. Lauren looked up and waved; but Rachel kept her head down, walking quickly to her next class. Immediately, Lauren started thinking about the worst-case scenarios:* Is Rachel mad at me? Why didn't she come over to talk to me—or at least wave back? What happened when I was with her last? Maybe I said something that offended her, or maybe she's just being a jerk. *Lauren walked on to class but couldn't stop thinking about how Rachel had acted. This interaction influenced her mood for the rest of the afternoon, making her crabby and anxious.*

Ask students to discuss the following questions in groups of three or four. Then, allow the groups to report their ideas to the larger group.

- *With which negative thought patterns does Lauren struggle?*
- *What could Lauren do to bring awareness to these negative thought patterns?*

Once the larger group has discussed the scenario, consider sharing some personal experiences with negative thought patterns (especially those not illustrated in the scenario). Offering personal examples can deepen the students' understanding and prepare them for the next exercise.

ALIVE (10-15 MINUTES)

In this section, you will encourage students to reflect on their own experiences with negative thought patterns. Bringing awareness to these patterns can offer new insight.

JOURNAL

Using the language in the next paragraph, invite the students to consider their own experiences and to spend some time writing or drawing in response to the prompts that follow.

> *Now that you are aware of some of these negative thought patterns, take a few moments to consider any of these patterns you have experienced. Choose one or two of the journal prompts in the Student Guide. Then, as you did last week, allow yourself time to write or draw without editing or erasing. We will spend five minutes responding to the prompts.*

Here are the prompts the students will find on pages 27–28 in the Student Guide:

- Which of these negative thought patterns have you experienced? Make a list, and then circle the patterns you experience most often.
- Describe a time when you have experienced one of these negative thought patterns.
- What situations can cause these types of thoughts in you? How do you typically respond when you start having negative thoughts?
- Describe a time when you noticed a friend or family member using one of these negative thought patterns. What did they do or say? How did you respond?

As you conclude the five minutes of journal time, encourage the students to continue exploring these questions and using the journal space in the Student Guide during the week. Then, invite them to talk about any reflections they feel comfortable sharing. Let students know that they may use what they wrote or drew as a guide and can share as much or as little as they want.

During the discussion, listen carefully to how your students describe their experiences and how they describe themselves. Notice when the students speak harshly about themselves, and take note of any negative self-talk (for example, *"I'm so weird." "It's kind of stupid, but . . ."*). While you don't want to call out any student by name, it may be helpful to share some of the phrases you heard during the discussion and observe that we are often unkind to ourselves.

If any of your students discuss the last prompt, you might point out your observations about the ways they respond differently to their friends' and family members' negative thought patterns than they do to their own, especially if they tend to show more compassion to others.

ABOUT SELF-COMPASSION

Self-compassion is essential to the way we talk to ourselves when negative thought patterns occur. You can read the paragraphs that follow to shift the discussion in a new direction, introducing the concept of self-compassion. (This text is also printed in the Student Guide on page 29.)

> In the greatest commandment in the New Testament, Jesus instructs us to love God with our whole being and to love our neighbor as ourselves. (See Matthew 22:36-39.) Yet all too often, loving ourselves and showing ourselves compassion is not something we practice. Instead, when we take time to notice our own thoughts, we often judge them or try to change them.
>
> Practicing self-compassion is crucial to mental and spiritual health. According to psychologist Kristin Neff, "Self-compassion is treating yourself with the same kindness, care, and concern you show a loved one."[4] Self-compassion does not mean hiding our flaws or ignoring our mistakes. Flaws and mistakes are what make us human! Neff suggests that we remind ourselves, "'I'm an imperfect human living an imperfect life.'"[5] When we practice self-compassion, we practice loving and forgiving ourselves the way that God loves and forgives us.

Conclude the discussion about negative thought patterns and self-compassion by asking the following question:

- *How might you show kindness and compassion to yourself when you recognize your own negative thought patterns? How can you greet negative thoughts with compassion and curiosity rather than judgment and fear?*

ABIDE (10–15 MINUTES)

AWARENESS MEDITATION WITH COMPASSION

In this section, students will repeat the awareness meditation; however, this time they will incorporate a mantra of compassion.

Mantras of Compassion

You may use the text that follows to guide the students to write their mantras.

A mantra is a short statement that you can repeat to yourself when you notice negative thoughts drawing you away from the present moment.

Allow students a few minutes to create mantras that remind them to practice self-compassion. You might offer a few examples: *Thoughts come and go; I do not have to believe everything I think.* Or *My thoughts do not define me; I am not alone; I am a child of God.* Students can write the mantra they choose in the blank circle on page 30 of the Student Guide.

Meditation with Compassion

Return to the awareness meditation that you practiced at the beginning of the session. Encourage students to try the practice again, adding an element of self-compassion. Read or paraphrase the paragraph that follows.

Meditation is not a onetime experience but a journey. We are going to practice again the awareness meditation, but this time we will incorporate our mantras of compassion. As we learn to quiet our minds and become more aware of our thoughts, remember that distractions and negative thought patterns are a part of life. Everyone has them. Practicing self-compassion here means letting go of judgment. Instead of trying to change these thoughts, we can observe them and move on.

Listen > *Week 2: Awareness Meditation*

Encourage students to use their mantras to help them release their thoughts and refocus on their breath as you repeat the "Awareness Meditation." You can use the audio track at UpperRoomBooks.com/TheAwakenedLife, or you can read the text found in the Awake section of this session.

Prayer

As the meditation ends, ask students to say this prayer with you. (It is located on page 30 of the Student Guide.)

> **God, help me to notice my own thoughts, to be thankful for my mind, and to love myself as you love me. Amen.**

Reflection

Invite the students to reflect on their experience of practicing the awareness meditation with compassion by recording their observations in Day 1 of the practice journal on page 32 of the Student Guide. Then, allow time for students to share their reflections with the group. You also might encourage students to respond to these questions:

- *How did you extend compassion to yourself during this meditation?*
- *How did this experience with the awareness meditation differ from the first?*

ARISE (5-10 MINUTES)

As you conclude, summarize the main points of the session and reiterate to the students the importance of doing the home practices. Read aloud or paraphrase these sentences (found in the Student Guide on page 31):

> *Today, you began to awaken to your mind and learned about the importance of self-compassion. Use the home practices this week to begin to get curious about how your mind works.*

Show the students where they can find the "Week 2: Awareness Meditation" audio track at UpperRoomBooks.com/TheAwakenedLife. Encourage students to try to extend the amount of time they spend in silence by adding a minute to their meditation practice each day. Also, remind them to keep a journal of their practices and to check in with their practice partners.

HOME PRACTICES FOR WEEK 2

1. Practice each day the awareness meditation *with compassion*. Start with three minutes. If that feels comfortable, challenge yourself the next day by adding a minute.

2. Keep track of your observations in the practice journal section of the Student Guide (beginning on page 32). For example, on Day 1, enter the date you practiced and the practice: "awareness meditation." Then, record anything you notice about your thoughts, emotions, and physical body. Keep in mind that there is no wrong answer.

3. Check in with your practice partner at least twice this week.

CLOSING BLESSING

Say the closing blessing together as you prepare to leave. (The blessing is printed in the Student Guide on page 31.)

We are awakening to abundant life.

We are becoming aware of our worth and belonging.

We are becoming alive to our senses, thoughts, and emotions.

We are abiding in the love and grace of God.

We arise now to live a life as connected, whole people.

WEEK 3

CONNECTING TO SELF

**BEING
PRESENT
IN THE
BODY**

MATERIALS

For this session, you will need the following items:

- Index cards
- Small sticky notes
- Markers
- Student Guides and/or journals
- Pens and pencils

LEADER PREPARATION

- **Review the full session**.
- **Create sensory element cards.** Prepare these cards to pass out during the Awake section. You will need one index card per student. On each card, write a different sense: *see*, *hear*, *smell*, *taste*, *feel*. Or you might use icons by drawing an eye, ear, nose, mouth, and hand. Make sure that all the senses are represented, repeating the list as necessary.
- **Locate the "Awakened Life" word wall.** If you have been building a word wall, make sure the students can access it again this week. You also may wish to provide a new color sticky note for this week.
- **Try the practice.** The Abide spiritual practice for this week is body prayer. We have provided you two options to consider, and we encourage you to explore these prayer practices before introducing one (or both) of them to your students. One option features several prayer postures and explores how these different positions might open us to different experiences of prayer. The second option includes a prayer sequence that pairs yoga postures with Psalm 46:10-11. (An alternative yoga prayer sequence, created by Jill Wondel, may be found online at UpperRoomBooks.com/TheAwakenedLife).

SCHEDULE FOR WEEK 3

 AWAKE (10–15 MINUTES)
    CHECK-IN
    INTRODUCTION

 AWARE (10–15 MINUTES)
    THE WHY
    JOURNAL

 ALIVE (10–15 MINUTES)
    MOVEMENT EXERCISES

 ABIDE (10–15 MINUTES)
    BODY PRAYERS

 ARISE (5–10 MINUTES)
    REVIEW HOME PRACTICES
    CLOSING BLESSING

AWAKE (10–15 MINUTES)

This week, you will encourage students to be present to their physical bodies and to become more aware of the ways in which we avoid or ignore the sensory input our bodies provide.

CHECK-IN

Begin this session with your group's check-in ritual; light a candle or say a prayer together. Then, ask about the home practices, using one or two of the prompts that follow.

This week, we awaken to the beauty and power of our bodies. Before we start, let's check in regarding your weekly practices.

- *What did you notice while practicing the awareness meditation at home? What observations did you record in your practice journal?*
- *What did you learn from connecting with your practice partner?*
- *What do you notice about your body right now?*

If you wish to walk your students through a short body scan to help them respond to the last question, you can prompt them with additional questions. For instance: Are you sitting up straight, or is your back rounded? Are both feet on the ground, or are your legs crossed? Are you holding tension anywhere? Check your neck, your jaw, your shoulders, or other places where you might carry stress.

INTRODUCTION TO WEEK 3: BEING PRESENT IN THE BODY

To introduce students to the theme, pass out the sensory element cards you created before the session. Give each student one card, making sure that each of the five senses will be addressed by at least one student. Then, read or paraphrase the following paragraphs. (This information is also found in the Student Guide on page 36.)

Have you ever taken time to marvel at the miracle of your own body? Your eyes perceive the smile of a friend, funny cat videos, and the majesty of the mountains. Your nose breathes in the smell of bread baking and the fragrance of a budding flower. Your ears soak in your own voice speaking your truth, your joyful singing in your car, and the precious moment when you hear the words "I love you." Your mouth open to the sweetness of honey and the pleasure of macaroni and cheese. Your skin intimately connects you to the delight of goose bump-inducing music, the power of clicking on a text message, and the shelter of a hug.

Pause here to ask students to read the sensory element on the card they received. Invite them to talk with one other person about a memorable experience they have with that sensory element. For instance, if a student received a "hear" card, he or she might describe a memory of an awesome concert or of a creaky stairwell that frightened him or her as a child—any strong memory related to the sensory element. Once you have given students a few minutes to share their sensory memories, ask partners to write on a sticky note a few words that summarize what they heard. Add these notes to the Awakened Life word wall, and then continue with the introduction.

> *Not only does your body make all these memorable experiences possible; it also allows you to connect with your mind and your soul. This mind-body-soul connection is crucial to wholeness. Your body signals you when you are hungry, tired, anxious, hurt, or sad. If you do not pay attention to these signals, your body becomes sluggish and cannot function properly. This disconnect can lead to spiraling thoughts that make it easier to forget that you are a precious child of God, designed with all the tools necessary to live abundantly. God's breath is in you, and you are "fearfully and wonder-fully made" (Ps. 139:14). You were created with the ability to know when you need to rest, nourish, heal, protect, and soothe your body. This week, you will focus on paying attention to what your body reveals to you about healthy ways to live. Again, this takes practice, but it is worth the effort.*

AWARE (10–15 MINUTES)

In this section, you will draw attention to the ways we numb or ignore our bodies and then invite students to write or draw about their own experiences.

THE WHY

Start by paraphrasing or reading aloud the following information. (This material is also printed in the Student Guide on pages 37–38.)

> *For some of us, staying "in the now," being present to all that is happen-ing in the moment, is seemingly impossible. Instead, we numb ourselves; we binge-watch videos or sports, gossip with friends, or log on to social media. Sometimes, we actively seek ways to avoid the present—when we*

are feeling anxious or lonely, procrastinating on homework, or dreading a tough conversation with a friend. Other times, we numb ourselves without realizing we are doing it; we reach for our smartphones to connect or scroll through social media without considering what "real-life" moments we might be missing.

Smartphone technology has many benefits; our smartphones have the potential to keep us connected to people and give us access to information and entertainment. However, many people report that phone use often isolates them from others as well as from what is happening in and around them. In a Psychology Today *article, a student shares his experience at dinner with some friends:*

> *Speaking of being tethered and isolating myself, just a few nights ago I went out to eat with my friends, and half the time we were at the restaurant I was constantly checking my phone; in fact I was too busy checking my own to even notice if anyone else had been looking at theirs. For some parts of the conversation I just gave short replies or nods to the conversation because I was missing what was actually being said. Even watching this video for class, I had to stop and rewind a few times because I found myself getting distracted by my phone.[1]*

After reading the excerpt from *Psychology Today,* take a minute to check in with your students. Ask them to answer the following questions with a thumbs up (*yes*) or thumbs down (*no*).

- *Does this story resonate with you?*
- *Has your phone ever been a distraction during meals, classes, or conversations with friends?*

Acknowledge that we all have ways that we "numb out" or avoid thoughts or feelings and the way they affect our bodies—if not by checking our phone, then in other ways. You might add a personal story about a time when you missed something important because you were "numbing out." Then, continue to read or paraphrase the following information.

Phone use can numb our senses. It can take us out of the present moment, causing us to miss out on what is happening around and in us. Avoiding the present has serious consequences for our bodies. Avoidance can make us anxious, and in turn, we carry this stress knowingly and unknowingly in our bodies.

Our bodies give us the best information about what is happening inside us right now; they connect us to the present. Instead of numbing and shutting out these messages, we can learn to sit with our own thoughts and feelings and to experience how they affect our bodies. The body signals its needs if we listen to it. For instance, our stomachs growl when we are hungry, and our eyes get heavy when we are tired. Listening to these signals and nourishing and taking care of our bodies can improve our physical, mental, and emotional health.

Acknowledge that often we don't notice or we ignore the signals our bodies give us. (You might offer an example: *Has your stomach ever growled and you thought,* I should eat, *but you didn't? Then, your thoughts began to spiral negatively, and you angrily snapped at a friend, who had done nothing wrong?*) Before you move into a time of personal reflection, you may want to share a story about a time when you did not listen to your body's cues.

JOURNAL

Invite students to reflect on their own experiences of numbing or ignoring body cues. Ask them to respond to one of the prompts that follow. (The prompts are also on pages 39–40 in the Student Guide.)

- Describe a time when you numbed yourself to avoid a situation. How did you "numb out"—perhaps by binge-watching Netflix or scrolling through social media? What were you avoiding—maybe a tough conversation or uncomfortable feelings (anxiety, loneliness, or guilt)? What did you miss out on? How did it affect your body?

- Describe a time when you did not listen to your body's signals. How did your body signal its needs? What happened when you ignored this signal? (Maybe you gave in to a negative thought pattern, or you snapped at a stranger.) What do you remember about your thoughts, emotions, and physical responses? If you could go back and pay attention to your body cues, how do you think the experience would be different?

Invite students to choose one prompt, and give them five minutes to respond. Then, allow time for students to talk in pairs about their responses.

NOTE FOR LEADERS: Responding to these journal prompts and talking about them even with one other person could be difficult for some students. Be aware of any students who have past experiences, such as abuse or an eating disorder, that might elicit a strong reaction. Allow them to pace themselves and to participate as much or as little as they are able.

ALIVE (10–15 MINUTES)

In this section you will invite students to participate in three short exercises that will get them moving. These exercises may be challenging for your group. "Thinking" with the body can be difficult for teens (and adults), but building physical awareness is important.

MOVEMENT EXERCISES

Encourage students to step outside of their comfort zone, and let them know you are taking the leap with them. Have fun with it. The more comfortable you are, the more comfortable your students will be.

Exercise 1

This "warm-up" exercise will help get everyone moving and focused on physical sensations. To guide students through the exercise, use the prompts that follow. (The prompts are also printed in the Student Guide on page 41.)

Clench your fists as tightly as you can, and hold them closed for fifteen seconds. . . . Now unclench them. Notice what you feel in your hands.

- *Describe the feeling.*
- *What sensations are you experiencing? Tingling? warmth? tension? other?*

Now smile for fifteen seconds. . . . Now relax your face.

- *Describe the feeling.*
- *How is this feeling different from what you felt after clenching your fists?*

Exercise 2

Once the students have completed the "warm-up," you might invite them to "act out" their response to some different scenarios. This exercise allows students to explore the ways we embody our thoughts and emotions.

Ask students to review the scenarios that follow. (This material is also printed in the Student Guide on page 41.)

- *You ate a whole bag of chips or a pint of ice cream by yourself.*
- *You stayed up all night playing on your phone.*
- *You partied too hard on Friday and missed a test prep session the next morning.*
- *You canceled a get-together with a friend and stayed home instead to binge-watch videos.*
- *You failed a quiz.*

After students have had an opportunity to review the list, read aloud the paragraph that follows.

> *Pick one of these scenarios. Take a few moments to think about how you would react. What might happen in your mind and body if this scenario occurred? How would you feel? What would you think? How would your body respond in relation to your thoughts and feelings?*

Rather than responding in words (writing or discussion), encourage students to respond with their bodies. Invite students to silently "act out" how they might think or feel in this scenario.

Especially if you have students who are shy, you might model the process and then invite all the students to provide their physical responses at the same time. You can then name what you observe. (*I see some downcast eyes. I see some shrugging shoulders and worried faces.*) Next, invite any students who feel comfortable to show their pose or to describe in words how they physically responded. You may use the following questions to suggest some possibilities.

> *Did you sink down in your chair and try to go unnoticed? Did your inner critic kick in and cause your jaw to tighten? Did a sense of self-loathing cause your body to slump? Did your hands clench in anger? Did you feel sick in the pit of your stomach? Or did you speak words of encouragement*

*to yourself, breathe deeply, and allow your tension to lessen? Did you
remind yourself that no one is perfect and stand a little taller?*

Remind students that we hold our thoughts and emotions in our bodies—whether we express them boldly or are unaware of them completely. We all face our own inner critics, and they can beat up on our bodies. But we can also demonstrate self-compassion and love in our bodies. This physical compassion can de-escalate feelings of stress and isolation.

Exercise 3

Introduce the "self-compassion selfie." Invite students to adopt a pose of self-compassion. Offer suggestions. For instance: "Use a hand to gently cradle your face," "Hug yourself," or "Place a comforting hand on your heart." Students can take a selfie, or they can work in pairs to snap photos of each other. Then, invite students to text the picture to their own phones, adding one or two sentences that express self-compassion and love.

This self-soothing exercise may feel strange to teens who are trying it for the first time. As the leader, you can help to normalize this activity and spark curiosity about trying something new. Let students know that the exercise may feel awkward at first but that loving yourself is a stepping stone to abundant life.

Reflection

These exercises should move quickly. Once the students have completed all three, allow time for a short reflection. You may use the following questions.

- *How did these exercises feel?*
- *Which exercise was the hardest for you? What made it difficult?*

As you wrap up this section, remind students to look at their selfies anytime they feel anxious and to read the words of self-compassion they sent to themselves.

ABIDE (10–15 MINUTES)

BODY PRAYERS

Now that the students have explored the connections between body, mind, and soul, they are prepared for this week's spiritual practice: body prayers. To introduce the practice, you may want to read aloud or paraphrase the paragraph that follows. (This material is also printed in the Student Guide on page 42.)

> *We often think of prayer as words spoken aloud or silently in our own minds. But when we think of prayer only as words, we downplay the importance of our physical posture. Our bodies can communicate what we are thinking and feeling; conversely, physical movement can help to shape our thoughts and feelings. For example, sometimes when we are in a bad mood, going for a walk can help change our perspective. Similarly, what we might have trouble expressing through words can sometimes be better expressed through our physical postures. Prayerful movement and postures can open us to receive new insights and understanding; they also enable us to express ourselves beyond words and to communicate with God in deeper ways.*

OPTION 1: Prayer Postures

Postures of prayer have been used by monks and nuns for centuries. Some of these postures are described in the Bible; others have been adopted over time. Here are just a few:

Kneeling with head bowed and hands folded

Standing with arms stretched upward, palms up

Sitting with head facing upward and both hands clasped over the heart

Lying prostrate (face down) on the ground with arms outstretched, forming a cross with the body

Sitting cross-legged, with a straight back, hands on thigh, palms open

Guide your students through these prayer postures in the same way you did with the warm-up exercise in the Alive section. (The postures are displayed in the Student Guide on page 43.) Before you begin, remind the students that these are prayerful postures. Then, ask the students to move as a group into each position as you describe it. Invite students to adopt the first posture and to hold it for fifteen seconds. Then, as they relax their bodies, ask them to describe how the posture felt. You may use these prompts.

- *How did you feel about adopting this posture?*
- *What thoughts or emotions did you experience while in this posture?*

Continue in this way until the students have experienced all the postures. Then, invite them to reflect on the experience of praying with their bodies, perhaps using the questions that follow. (The questions are in the Student Guide on page 43.) This can be a group discussion, or you can ask students to write their responses in the Day 1 section of the practice journal on page 46 of the Student Guide.

- *What other postures might communicate your thoughts and feelings to God?*
- *What new prayer postures might you add to this list?*

OPTION 2: Body Movement

In this option, you will guide your students through the body movement sequence that follows. (This sequence is also located at UpperRoomBooks.com/TheAwakenedLife and in the Student Guide on page 44.) This form of body prayer pairs a sequence of yoga poses with the words of Psalm 46:10-11. Introduce your students to the five poses in the sequence, and then practice each one together. Remind them that these are prayerful poses. Next, invite the students to hold each pose as you read the corresponding lines of the psalm. Finally, encourage the students to flow through the entire sequence as you read aloud Psalm 46:10-11.

"Be still, and know that I am God!

I am exalted among the nations,

I am exalted in the earth."

The Lᴏʀᴅ of hosts is with us;

the God of Jacob is our refuge.

After the students learn the body movement sequence, invite them to reflect on the experience of praying with their bodies by responding to the questions that follow. (These prompts are printed in the Student Guide on page 44.) This can be a group discussion, or you can ask students to write their responses in the Day 1 section of the practice journal on page 46 of the Student Guide.

- *What thoughts or emotions did you experience while adopting each pose?*
- *How do you usually pray? How does this experience compare?*

Encourage students to try a body prayer each day during the week. They can use the prayer posture or body movement prayer they practiced today, try a different body movement prayer (with yoga sequence) available at UpperRoomBooks.com/TheAwakenedLife, or create a new prayer each day by combining postures or poses.

ARISE (5-10 MINUTES)

Read or paraphrase the lines that follow to summarize the key ideas of this session. Then, reiterate the importance of doing the home practice and journaling each day. Answer any questions students may have about the home practice before they leave.

Today, you began to awaken to your physical body and became more aware of the ways you often avoid or ignore the sensory input your body provides.

HOME PRACTICE FOR WEEK 3

1. Try the Abide spiritual practice (body prayer) each day. You can repeat the body prayer from the session, try a new one available at UpperRoomBooks.com/TheAwakenedLife, or create your own by combining two or three prayer postures or yoga poses, perhaps to accompany a favorite scripture passage.

2. Keep track of your observations in the practice journal section of the Student Guide (beginning on page 46). For example, on Day 1, enter the date you practiced and the practice: "body prayer." Then, record anything you notice about your thoughts, emotions, and physical body. Keep in mind that there is no wrong answer.

3. Check in with your practice partner at least twice this week. You may want to create a body prayer sequence and practice it together.

CLOSING BLESSING

Say the closing blessing in unison as you conclude the session. (The blessing is printed in the Student Guide on page 45.)

We are awakening to abundant life.

We are becoming aware of our worth and belonging.

We are becoming alive to our senses, thoughts, and emotions.

We are abiding in the love and grace of God.

We arise now to live a life as connected, whole people.

WEEK 4

CONNECTING TO OTHERS

WORKING THROUGH LONELINESS

MATERIALS

For this session, you will need the following items:

- Small sticky notes
- Markers
- Internet access, computer, and speakers (optional)
- Student Guides and/or journals
- Pens and pencils

LEADER PREPARATION

- **Review the full session**.
- **Locate the "Awakened Life" word wall.** If you have been building a word wall, make sure the students can access it again this week. You also may wish to provide a new color sticky note for this week.
- **Try the practice.** The Awake and Abide sections incorporate a meditation practice ("Loving-Kindness Meditation"). We encourage you to try it yourself before presenting it to your students. You can use the audio tracks "Week 4: Loving-Kindness Meditation 1" and "Week 4: Loving-Kindness Meditation 2" at UpperRoomBooks.com/TheAwakenedLife.
- **Research Parker Palmer's Circle of Trust Touchstones**. The deep listening exercise included in the Alive section incorporates some of the core components of Palmer's Touchstones. Before you lead this session, you may want to review the Touchstones on his website at www.couragerenewal.org/touchstones.
- **Prepare for the love feast in Week 5.** Next week, the group will be celebrating a love feast. Start planning now, using the information in the Materials, Leader Preparation, and Abide sections of Week 5; gather

supplies, become familiar with the love feast liturgy, and invite students to be involved in planning and leadership. If you plan to ask a student to bake bread for the service, be sure to give him or her plenty of notice.

SCHEDULE FOR WEEK 4

 AWAKE (10–15 MINUTES)
CHECK-IN
INTRODUCTION
LOVING-KINDNESS MEDITATION

 AWARE (5 MINUTES)
THE WHY

 ALIVE (20–25 MINUTES)
JOURNAL
DEEP LISTENING EXERCISE

 ABIDE (5–10 MINUTES)
LOVING-KINDNESS MEDITATION

 ARISE (5–10 MINUTES)
REVIEW HOME PRACTICES
CLOSING BLESSING

AWAKE (10–15 MINUTES)

For the past few weeks, students have been forging connections with the self (mind and body). The next two weeks center on our connections with others. This week, in particular, invites students to explore loneliness or the feeling of disconnection. The Awake section sets the stage to talk about the importance of relationships.

CHECK-IN

First, as in previous weeks, take time to signal the beginning of your sacred time together by lighting a candle or saying a prayer together. Then, ask about the home practices, using one or two of the prompts that follow.

- *What observations did you make in your practice journal this week? During the last session we talked about becoming more aware of our bodies and the ways they connect us to the present moment. As you read and reflect on your journal entries, what do you notice about your body right now?*

- *Last week, we also thought about the ways our bodies can communicate our thoughts and feelings. As we begin our session today, how are you feeling?*

  Ask students to take a pose that expresses how they feel today. Then, pass out sticky notes. Invite students to draw their pose (stick figures are fine!) or to write a word or phrase that could sum up their pose. Encourage the students to add their sticky notes to the word wall.

- *How did you connect with your practice partner this week? How has your relationship changed over the past three weeks?*

INTRODUCTION TO WEEK 4: WORKING THROUGH LONELINESS

To provide a transition into the new content for this week, paraphrase or read aloud the paragraphs that follow. (They are also printed in the Student Guide on page 50.)

Over the last three weeks, you began awakening to God's presence in your mind and body. By listening to your own thoughts and feelings, you are beginning to extend compassion to yourself. By quieting negative thoughts and diminishing the distractions, you are creating space to experience an awakened and abundant life. Hopefully, you are realizing or remembering that you are a beloved child of God who is held in grace. God's grace is the unconditional love and transforming power given freely to you and available in each moment.

Our next step is connecting to other people. As you quiet your mind and extend compassion to yourself, you can begin to make space for others. As you recognize that you are a beloved child of God, you also realize that God's love extends to everyone. As you sense God working in and through you, you can celebrate the ways God also is working in and through other people. As you embrace your own worth, you can acknowledge the worth of others and build meaningful relationships.

LOVING-KINDNESS MEDITATION

The practice for this week is loving-kindness meditation. You may introduce the practice by reading aloud or paraphrasing the paragraph that follows. (It is also in the Student Guide on page 50.)

We are created to be in relationship with one another. Being present with others, like being awake and present to ourselves, is a skill we develop over years. This week, we will practice loving-kindness meditation. We will begin by offering loving-kindness to ourselves, and then we will extend that loving-kindness to others.

We are going to try it together now, and we will practice it again at the end of our session today. Then, you will be invited to practice this meditation on your own during the week.

Listen > *Week 4: Loving-Kindness Meditation 1*

To guide your students through the meditation, use the script that follows or the audio track "Week 4: Loving-Kindness Meditation 1" at UpperRoomBooks.com/TheAwakenedLife. If you use the script, be sure to read slowly and with intention; give students space to pause and to notice their breath and thoughts.

Sit comfortably in an upright position, and take a few moments to notice your breath and your body. As we have done in previous weeks, begin by focusing on your breath. Notice your breath in this moment. Imagine breathing in loving warmth and energy and breathing out anything that is keeping you from being present. Take a moment to be with your breath. Next, notice any areas of your body that might be holding tension, and gently relax those areas.

As we begin, start by tuning in to a sense of softness and compassion for yourself. Then, simply repeat to yourself these five phrases as I read them aloud.

May I feel safe.
May I be happy.
May I know the joy of being alive.
May I be filled with loving-kindness.
May I be free.

As you continue to repeat each phrase in your mind, notice what images or feelings arise in you. Pay attention to what happens in your body. Imagine treating yourself as you would your best friend. This might be difficult for you, but continue to imagine having this kind of love for yourself.

Now, think of someone whom you love very much. Think of the qualities that you admire about your loved one. Reflect on the things that you most appreciate about who this person is. Begin to extend loving-kindness to this person as you repeat to yourself the phrases I read aloud. You may replace "they" with this person's name.

May they feel safe.
May they be happy.
May they know the joy of being alive.
May they be filled with loving-kindness.
May they be free.

Prayer

As the meditation ends, ask students to say this prayer with you. (It is printed on page 51 of the Student Guide.)

> **God, help me to be fully present and thankful for the opportunity to share life with the people in this group. Amen.**

Reflection

To debrief the practice with your students, consider using the following prompts.

- *How did you feel while participating in this practice?*
- *What do you need to let go of so that you can be fully present?*

AWARE (5 MINUTES)

In this section, you will teach students about the pervasiveness of loneliness and the way it affects our mental, emotional, and spiritual health.

THE WHY

Take a moment to read aloud to the group the paragraphs that follow. (This information is also in the Student Guide on pages 51–52.)

> *Have you ever felt lonely in a crowded room? Have you ever felt lonely sitting with friends who are on their phones? Have you opened your phone to connect, but wound up feeling more alone as you scrolled through social media? Loneliness does not necessarily mean being alone but feeling alone. Loneliness is a feeling of disconnection—a feeling that no one "gets" you or that you do not have the meaningful relationships you would like to have.*
>
> *If you feel lonely, you are not the only one feeling that way. A recent study (BBC's Loneliness Experiment) found that levels of loneliness are*

highest among sixteen-to-twenty-four-year-olds. More than 40 percent of young people said they often feel lonely, compared to 27 percent of people over the age of seventy-five.[1] Four out of ten young people surveyed said they often felt misunderstood, sad, detached, and like they did not have anyone to talk with. Another study showed that the number of teens who feel lonely has increased over the past decade; in 2017, 39 percent of high school seniors said they often felt lonely, compared to 26 percent in 2012.[2]

If you feel lonely and disconnected, you can do something about it. Meaningful relationships are beautiful and messy. They take effort, but they are worth the investment and can lead to experiences of love, respect, and connection. Did you know science has proven that when individuals sing a song in a choir, the hearts of the singers begin to beat as one in rhythm with the music and with one another?[3] Interconnection is possible and real.

ALIVE (20-25 MINUTES)

In this section, you will help the students explore their own experiences with connection and disconnection. After they have responded to journal prompts for about five minutes, ask them to break into pairs for the Deep Listening Exercise.

JOURNAL

Invite the students to think about times they have felt connected or disconnected. Then, ask them to read the journal prompts on pages 53–55 in the Student Guide, the same prompts that follow here. Allow five minutes for students to write their responses to one or two of the prompts. Let them know that the group will continue to explore these questions in the next exercise.

- Describe a time when you experienced a feeling of deep connection with
  — a family member.
  — a girlfriend or boyfriend.
  — a friend.
  — a teacher or coach.

- Describe a time when you experienced disconnection and/or conflict with
  — a family member.
  — a girlfriend or boyfriend.
  — a friend.
  — a teacher or coach.

- Describe the feeling of connection. How does your body respond to connection? What kinds of things do you tell yourself when you feel connected?

- Describe the feeling of disconnection or loneliness. How does your body respond to loneliness? What kinds of things do you tell yourself when you are lonely?

DEEP LISTENING EXERCISE

When the students complete their individual reflection, read or paraphrase the following paragraph to provide a transition into the group exercise. (This text is also in the Student Guide on page 56.)

Connection in any relationship happens when we make space to hear the other person and when we are heard. This means listening to everything from the mundane details of everyday life to big dreams for the future. Listening—and truly hearing—also allows us to lean into conflict, leading to growth as we learn from moments of disconnection.

This Deep Listening Exercise gives students the opportunity to be fully present to one another as they share deeply. Emphasize the importance of being present and listening quietly, without fixing. You can provide an overview of the deep listening exercise by reading or paraphrasing the following paragraph.

Let's take some time to practice deep listening. In a moment, I will ask each of you to find a partner and to move to a place where you can sit face-to-face. One person will speak for three minutes, without interruption, about a personal experience of feeling connected or disconnected. Then, partners will switch roles and repeat the exercise so that each person has a chance to share and be heard. When your partner is speaking, try not to get distracted or to ask questions; simply listen as closely as possible.

Guidelines

Before the students pair up, walk them through the guidelines for deep listening that follow.[4] In particular, you will want to emphasize the importance of confidentiality. (The guidelines are printed in the Student Guide on pages 56–57.)

Listeners, here are some key things to know and remember:

- Your role is to be quiet and present.
- Hold in confidence what you hear; trust is crucial.

- You do not need to fix anything or to offer advice. Just listen.
- Be curious about and open to what you hear.
- If your mind wanders, gently reengage in listening. Remember: People deserve to be heard.

Speakers, here are some key things to know and remember:

- You are *invited* to share but not forced. If you do not wish to share or if you run out of things to say during your three minutes, you can opt for silence.
- This is a safe place. What you choose to say will be held in confidence.
- Speak from your own experience. Focus on your own thoughts and emotions rather than those of others.
- Respect the experiences of others. Avoid name-calling and debating. Be respectful of your listener as well as of the person about whom you are speaking.
- Sharing your story is a powerful opportunity for healing.

Once students understand the guidelines, invite each of them to find a partner and to take turns talking about an experience of connection or disconnection. You may want to offer this prompt to clarify their task: *Describe to your partner a time when you experienced a feeling of deep connection or a feeling of disconnection with a family member, a boyfriend or girlfriend, a friend, or a teacher.* Allow six minutes for this exercise. Consider timing each speaker for three minutes to ensure each student has an equal turn to speak and to listen.

Reflection

When each student has had the opportunity to speak and to listen, you can help the group to debrief the experience. Keep the focus on the practice of deep listening rather than on the individual experiences of connection and disconnection that the students have shared. To facilitate the discussion, you may use these prompts:

- *Describe how you felt being the listener.*
- *Describe how you felt being the speaker.*
- *How might this deep listening practice help your relationships?*

ABIDE (5–10 MINUTES)

LOVING-KINDNESS MEDITATION

In this section, you will invite students to revisit the loving-kindness meditation and to expand it to include not only someone they love but also someone with whom they are in conflict. You can use the paragraph that follows to explain this additional step in the practice.

> *We are going to practice loving-kindness meditation again, and this time we are going to expand the practice. We will start in the same way, offering kindness and love to ourselves and extending kindness to someone we love. Then, we will practice sending loving-kindness to someone with whom we are in conflict. Notice the thoughts and emotions you experience during this meditation without placing pressure or judgment on yourself. If extending loving-kindness to someone with whom you are in conflict becomes uncomfortable, simply return to the practice of extending kindness to someone you love.*

Listen > *Week 4: Loving-Kindness Meditation 2*

To guide the students through the meditation, play the audio track "Week 4: Loving-Kindness Meditation 2" at UpperRoomBooks.com/TheAwakenedLife or read aloud the script that follows. If you use the script, remember to read slowly and with intention.

> *Sit comfortably in an upright position, and take a few moments to get in touch with your breath and your body. Begin by focusing on your breath. Notice your breath in this moment. Imagine breathing in loving warmth and energy and breathing out anything that is keeping you from being present. Take a moment to be with your breath. Next, notice any areas of your body that might be holding tension, and gently relax these areas. Begin by tuning in to a sense of softness and compassion for yourself. Then, simply repeat to yourself these five phrases as I read them aloud.*

May I feel safe.
May I be happy.
May I know the joy of being alive.
May I be filled with loving-kindness.
May I be free.

Now, bring to mind someone you love very much or someone to whom you feel deeply connected. Think of the qualities that you admire about your loved one. Reflect on the things that you most appreciate about who this person is. Begin to extend loving-kindness to this person as you repeat silently the phrases I read aloud. You may replace "they" with this person's name. Notice any images or feelings that arise within you.

May they feel safe.
May they be happy.
May they know the joy of being alive.
May they be filled with loving-kindness.
May they be free.

Now, if you are able, think of someone who has hurt or offended you—someone with whom you are in conflict or with whom you have a troubled or difficult relationship. Bring this person's face to mind. Begin to extend loving-kindness to this person as you repeat in your mind the phrases I read aloud. You may replace "they" with this person's name. Notice what thoughts and feelings arise within you. If this becomes too uncomfortable, you can return your focus to the practice of extending kindness to someone you love.

May they feel safe.
May they be happy.
May they know the joy of being alive.

May they be filled with loving-kindness.
May they be free.

Prayer

Invite the students to say this prayer together as you end the loving-kindness meditation. (The prayer is printed on page 58 of the Student Guide.)

God, help me to be fully present to what you are doing in and through me this week. Amen.

Reflection

Encourage the students to reflect on their experience of this expanded practice by using the prompts that follow. You might ask them to write their responses in Day 1 of the practice journal for this week (found on page 60 of the Student Guide).

- *What did you experience during this expanded loving-kindness meditation?*
- *How did you feel extending loving-kindness to someone with whom you are in conflict or have a difficult relationship?*

ARISE (5–10 MINUTES)

Continue to reinforce the daily practices, and encourage students to record their experiences in their practice journals. Invite students to practice deep listening this week as well as loving-kindness meditation. You might read aloud the sentences that follow.

Today, you expanded beyond self as you began to awaken to your connection with others. You practiced loving-kindness meditation and deep listening techniques. Use these practices this week to begin to strengthen and deepen your connection to others.

HOME PRACTICES FOR WEEK 4

1. Try the Abide spiritual practice (loving-kindness meditation) each day.

2. Keep track of your observations in the practice journal section of the Student Guide (beginning on page 60). For example, on Day 1, enter the date you practiced and the practice: "loving-kindness meditation." Then, record anything you notice about your thoughts, emotions, and physical body. Keep in mind that there is no wrong answer.

3. Check in with your practice partner at least twice this week. You may want to practice together the deep listening exercise and the loving-kindness meditation.

4. Consciously practice deep listening in your everyday conversations this week.

CLOSING BLESSING

Say together the closing blessing as you prepare to leave. (The blessing is printed in the Student Guide on page 59.)

We are awakening to abundant life.

We are becoming aware of our worth and belonging.

We are becoming alive to our senses, thoughts, and emotions.

We are abiding in the love and grace of God.

We arise now to live a life as connected, whole people.

WEEK 5

CONNECTING TO OTHERS

WORKING THROUGH SHAME

MATERIALS

For this session, you will need the following items:

- Small sticky notes
- Markers
- Internet access, computer, screen, and speakers
- Student Guides and/or journals
- Pens and pencils
- Dissolving paper (available from science stores or online from Amazon)
- Large glass or clear bowl filled with water
- Items for the love feast—bread, a pitcher of ice water, a large candle, matches, a bread basket, small plates, cups, and napkins. (Consider providing a gluten-free bread option.)

LEADER PREPARATION

- **Review the full session**.
- **Locate the "Awakened Life" word wall.** If you have been building a word wall, make sure the students can access it this week. You also may wish to provide a new color sticky note for this week.
- **Preview the online content**. The Aware section incorporates a TEDx video of Brené Brown called "The Power of Vulnerability." It is available at UpperRoomBooks.com/TheAwakenedLife or https://www.ted.com/talks/brene_brown_on_vulnerability. Watch the video before the session to familiarize yourself with the content. To ensure you have enough time to complete the other activities in this session, we recommend that you show your students an abbreviated clip (minutes 3:14–11:10 and 19–20) of the full talk. But you can decide what portion is best for your students or if you

would rather just paraphrase the big ideas. You can show this video to the whole group on a large screen or have the students watch the video on their phones in small groups if this is easier.

- **Prepare for the love feast.** This session ends with the group's celebrating a love feast. Read through the service in the Abide section of this session. Consider the ways your students can be involved in leadership—reading the liturgy, planning and leading music, sharing stories, setting the table, and baking bread. You will want to assign leadership roles ahead of time so that students are aware of what they are being asked to read or contribute. Identify three Readers, and ask them to review the love feast liturgy (printed in the Student Guide on pages 70–74); consider rehearsing the service with them as well. You will want to set up a large table and chairs so that your group can enjoy this meal together around the table. You can set a small plate, a cup, and a napkin at each place. You will also need a candle (and matches), a serving basket for the bread, and a pitcher of ice water. Unlike typical Communion bread, the bread for this meal can be a loaf of ordinary bread, rolls, or a sweet bread (baked perhaps by one of your students). The beverage for this meal is water, which can be poured from a pitcher into individual cups. (You can learn more about the love feast at https://www.umcdiscipleship.org/resources/the-love-feast.)

- **Make plans for the prayer walk in Week 6.** Next week, the group will be practicing a walking meditation. This prayer walk is intended to take place outside, preferably in a natural setting. You might arrange to hold the session at a local park, nature preserve, community garden, or farm. Or you might want to scout out an appropriate spot on or near the church property. If the weather is not suitable for a nature walk, you might create an indoor walking space that incorporates natural elements. Start planning for the prayer walk now. If you plan to meet the students at a remote location, be sure to communicate this information to the students and to their parents this week.

SCHEDULE FOR WEEK 5

 AWAKE (5–10 MINUTES)
CHECK-IN
LOVING-KINDNESS MEDITATION (OPTIONAL)
INTRODUCTION

 AWARE (10–15 MINUTES)
THE WHY

 ALIVE (15–20 MINUTES)
JOURNAL
COURAGEOUS CONVERSATIONS

 ABIDE (10–15 MINUTES)
LOVE FEAST

 ARISE (5–10 MINUTES)
REVIEW HOME PRACTICES
CLOSING BLESSING

AWAKE (5-10 MINUTES)

CHECK-IN

As students enter the room, ask them to take a sticky note and to write on it the answer to the prompt that follows. Then, invite students to add their sticky notes to the "Awakened Life" word wall.

- *With whom did you sense a connection as you practiced deep listening this week? On your sticky note, write the person's name or an insight you learned from that person.*

Next, ask students to review their home practice journals and to share reflections about loving-kindness meditation. (If you have time, you might invite the students to practice the meditation together again before you introduce Week 5. You can use the instructions printed in the Abide section of Week 4 or listen to the audio track "Week 4: Loving-Kindness Meditation 2" found at UpperRoomBooks.com/TheAwakenedLife.) Be sure to let students know that they will be asked to continue exploring loving-kindness meditation as their home practice for another week.

INTRODUCTION TO WEEK 5: WORKING THROUGH SHAME

After the check-in, read aloud the paragraph that follows. (This paragraph can also be found in the Student Guide on page 64.)

> *Imagine waking up in the morning embraced by divine love. This love provides an unshakable sense of worthiness and belonging. It gives you the courage to know and be known by other people. Imagine being exactly who God created you to be. Authenticity is a gift to others. It enables you to be a great friend because you have empathy and compassion to share. Imagine loving with your whole heart and celebrating with gratitude and joy the knowledge that you are enough. This vision can become a reality in your life. Communion with God and others is possible. This connection is key to the abundant life we have been seeking throughout our weeks together.*

AWARE (10–15 MINUTES)

In this section, you will help students understand how shame can keep us from connection. Brené Brown's TEDx talk entitled "The Power of Vulnerability" offers a clear explanation of this concept. Be aware that this session covers a lot of material, and the complete video requires about twenty minutes. You may want to show your students an abbreviated clip of the longer video. We recommend that you start the video at three minutes and fourteen seconds and stop at eleven minutes and ten seconds; then, pick up at minute nineteen and watch through the end of the video.

THE WHY

Before you share the video with your students, you may want to introduce Brené Brown by reading aloud or paraphrasing the paragraph that follows. (This information can be found on page 65 of the Student Guide.)

> *We are going to watch a TEDx talk by Dr. Brené Brown. Dr. Brown is a social work researcher; she collects people's stories and studies them to learn about human behavior. In this talk, she describes her insights into connection and what can help us form or hold us back from meaningful relationships.*

Watch > *Brené Brown, "The Power of Vulnerability", TEDx*

The TEDx talk is available at UpperRoomBooks.com/TheAwakenedLife or https://www.ted.com/talks/brene_brown_on_vulnerability.

After you watch the video, ask your students to identify the parts of the talk that stood out to them. Then, explain that in this session you will be focusing on Brené Brown's ideas about shame. You might read aloud or paraphrase the paragraphs that follows. (This material can be found in the Student Guide on page 65.)

> *We all have felt shame before. We all have felt as if we aren't good enough, smart enough, or strong enough. Shame is a universal experience. But sadly, it can keep us from being vulnerable and real with others; shame can hold us back from connection.*
>
> *It is important to note the difference between guilt and shame: Guilt is thinking,* I did something bad, *while shame is thinking,* I am bad.[1] *Guilt helps us realize that we have acted in a way that does not live up to our*

values and, as a result, have caused hurt. Guilt challenges us to ask for forgiveness and to make a change; it creates an opportunity for growth. Shame, on the other hand, leads us to feel unworthy. If we continually think people will not love the real us, we may begin to feel lonely and isolated. Shame can paralyze us.

You might provide students with a general example of guilt extending into shame to ensure they understand the idea. (For example: If I failed my English exam, I might feel *guilty* for not studying. However, if I allow my guilt to lead me to believe that I failed because I am not smart enough, I begin to feel *shame*: I failed my exam because *I* am a failure.) Also, if you feel comfortable doing so, share from your own experience a similar example of guilt that led to shame and how you realized that your thinking was controlling the way you felt about yourself. Your openness will help to prepare the students to move into a time of identifying their own experiences with guilt and shame.

ALIVE (15-20 MINUTES)

In this section, you will invite students to spend some time reflecting on shame and then to participate in a small-group discussion. Shame might be a difficult topic for some students, and these exercises may elicit complex feelings. Be sensitive to body language and to the feelings that come up in the group; allow time and space to process these feelings. Remember to *invite* students to participate rather than *demand* that they participate. (You might want to read again the "How to Talk About Difficult Topics" section on page 12 of "Getting Started" as you plan ways to handle issues that might arise in this session.)

JOURNAL

To begin, you may read aloud or paraphrase the following paragraph to invite students to reflect on their own experiences with shame.

> *Take a few moments to process your own experience with guilt and shame. Try to be open and honest as you respond to prompts and questions, knowing that your reflections will remain private unless you choose to share them.*

Read aloud the prompts that follow, and encourage students to choose a couple prompts or questions that they would like to respond to on pages 66–68 of the Student Guide. Invite students to write or draw—whichever they prefer. Let them know they are free to stretch or walk around the room as long as they don't disturb the reflection of other students.

- Write in the space below all the ways you would complete this sentence: "I am not _____ enough." How does your body respond when you write these words?
- How do you speak to yourself when you feel ashamed because you are not _____ enough? What do you say?
- Young people often experience shame in relation to issues such as body image or showing emotion. What issues have led you to feel shame? What parts of yourself do you want to hide from other people?
- If shame were an animal, what would it look like?

- Describe a time when you were vulnerable and let people see your imperfections. Who or what gave you the courage to be who you truly are? What happened as a result?
- Describe a time when you responded to your own feelings of shame and unworthiness with kindness and compassion. In what ways did that change how you see yourself?

Allow five to ten minutes for students to write or draw responses to the prompts they chose. Then, encourage them to continue responding to the prompts at home during the week.

COURAGEOUS CONVERSATIONS

As a leader, you will need to decide how best to prepare your group for this exercise. Acknowledge the difficulty of telling others about our feelings of shame and unworthiness, but also affirm the release that comes when we no longer have to hide these feelings. When we bring our shame into the light, it loses its power over us. When we share these feelings of shame and unworthiness with one another, we build trust and connection. Together, we can help one another to see that we are more than the negative things we might think about ourselves. Encourage students to exercise self-compassion as they muster the courage to open up, perhaps by repeating the mantra of compassion they created in Week 2.

You might introduce students to this time of courageous conversations by reading aloud the paragraph that follows and adding your own words of support and encouragement.

> *Shame grows in secrecy, silence, and judgment.*[2] *These next moments of conversation are crucial to overcoming shame and allowing for connection with others. They will require vulnerability and authenticity. Remember that this group is a space of deep listening—free of judgment and advice-giving. Sharing our stories can be powerful and healing.*

Instructions

Invite each student to find a partner. For this exercise, consider asking practice partners to work together since they have been sharing more deeply throughout the study. Give each pair two pens and two pieces of dissolvable paper. (Do not yet tell students that the paper will dissolve.) Then, ask partners to move to a place in the room where they can talk privately.

Explain that you will invite each student to bring to light an example of shame in one of two ways. Students can write on a piece of paper one of ways they completed this prompt: "I am not _____ enough." Or they can use words, pictures, or symbols to express on a piece of paper how their shame looks or feels to them. Next, you will ask students to risk sharing with their partners what they have drawn or written; then, you will invite partners, if they feel comfortable, to share more details about their experiences with shame. Be sure to remind the students that they are invited to share, but they are not required to say more than they are comfortable revealing. This might also be a good time to remind students about the importance of confidentiality and safety within the group.

Also, remind students to offer support when they are listening to a partner. A listener's job is not to make the speaker feel better; rather, a listener's job is simply to be with the person in his or her experience. You can suggest that partners respond to each other by speaking words of affirmation: "You are enough." "You are courageous." "You are loved."

When everyone understands the exercise, invite students to use the instructions on page 69 in the Student Guide to help them express on paper an example of shame and to share with and respond to their partner. (The guidelines are printed here for your reference.)

- Write or draw on a piece of paper either a picture of the way your shame looks or feels to you OR one of the ways way you completed this sentence: "I am not _____ enough."

- **Speakers**, share with your partner what you wrote or drew on your paper. Then, if you wish, take a few moments to say anything else you would like to add about your experience with shame.

- **Listeners**, practice deep listening as your partner speaks. Your task is not to "fix" your partner; you cannot erase the experience of shame or minimize its pain. Simply be with the person; offer your listening ear and support. You might respond to your partner with words of affirmation: "You are enough." "You are courageous." "You are loved."

Reflection

While partners are talking, place a large bowl of water on a table. Once all the partners have had the opportunity to speak and to listen, ask them to come back together as a group and to bring their papers with them. Ask students to reflect on the exercise by responding to the question that follows. Be sensitive to the difficulties that students might express, and affirm the courage they showed in taking this risk to open up.

- *How did you feel while talking about shame with other people?*

Dissolving Shame

Then, read or paraphrase the paragraph that follows to invite students to engage in a visual expression of their desire to release the hold that shame has in their lives.

> *Being vulnerable and naming our shame are acts of courage that can defeat shame. By practicing these courageous conversations with people we trust, we can learn to recognize the spiraling thoughts that lead to shame. With faith and self-compassion, we can begin to break the power of shame in our lives. If this is your desire, I invite you and your partner to come forward and drop your papers into the water.*

Encourage partners to come forward together, to drop into the water the papers they wrote on earlier, and to watch them dissolve and disappear. Then, you might use the paragraph that follows as a blessing, reiterating the words you used to open this session and shifting the focus to the love feast celebration.

> *We do not have to hide in shame. Communion with God and connection with others is not only possible; it also opens the way to the abundant life we are seeking. Each of us is embraced by divine love. This love provides an unshakable sense of worthiness and belonging. It instills in us the courage and the desire to know and be known by other people. It enables us to show empathy and compassion, to be a good friend. It empowers us to love with our whole heart. Being who God created us to be is a gift to*

others. Be grateful and joyful in the knowledge that you are enough. You are courageous. You are loved. Let's celebrate that!

ABIDE (10–15 MINUTES)

LOVE FEAST

To introduce the love feast, you may read aloud the paragraphs that follow. Then, invite the students to bring their Student Guides and to sit around the table that has been prepared.

> *Our spiritual practice for the week is a form of communion—a deep connection with God and with one another. We will celebrate our connection to God and others with a love feast. The love feast is a Christian tradition that recalls the meals Jesus shared with his disciples and honors the community and fellowship we share as the body of Christ. All are welcome at this table.*
>
> *Originally, this feast was known as the agape meal, echoing the Greek word for "self-giving love" in the New Testament. The setting and symbols of the love feast may remind you of the sacrament of Holy Communion, but these two services are quite distinct. The love feast is a service of sharing food, prayer, hymns, and faith stories. It is a more informal service in which group participation and shared leadership are encouraged. Participants are invited to tell stories of what God is doing in their lives, and children and teens often are involved in leadership.*
>
> *Welcome to this table of belonging, acceptance, and love, where we can find courage to know and be known by God and one another. In Christ, God receives us as we are and calls us enough—and not only enough but blessed with God's love and the company of friends.*

Instructions

To provide instructions for the love feast, you may read aloud or paraphrase the paragraph that follows. Invite students to join in the liturgy that starts on page 71 in the Student Guide.

As we sit around the table, we will read the love feast liturgy responsively as a group. I, as the Leader, and those of you who agreed to be Readers will read the words in italics; *the group will read together the words in* **bold italics**. *During the liturgy, we will share a meal of bread and water. We will pass the bread around the table, and each person will hold the basket of bread while the next person at the table takes a piece. In the same way, we will pass the pitcher around the table, pouring a cup of water for the person next to us. As you serve the person next to you, you may offer a blessing by saying the person's name and adding words such as these:*

- *Bread: "[Insert Person's Name], the gift of life and strength."*
- *Water: "[Insert Person's Name], the promise of abundant life."*

After everyone receives the bread and water, we will have a blessing and enjoy our meal together. During the meal, you will be invited to share stories of the ways you have seen God at work recently—in your life, in the lives of others in the group, or in the world. Then, we will close with music and prayer.

CELEBRATING THE LOVE FEAST

Blessing the Gathering

READER 1: *"How good and pleasant it is when God's people live together in unity!"* (Ps. 133:1, NIV). *Welcome to this meal. We come to share in God's love.*

ALL: *We come to share our food and our lives.*

READER 2: *We come to break bread together and to open ourselves to one another.*

ALL: *We come to express our faith and our thanks.*

READER 3: We come to taste the living water and to offer our lives in gratitude.

ALL: *May God bless this food and our fellowship.*

Opening Music

(Choose a song of invitation and praise, such as "Be Present at Our Table, Lord" or "The Lord's Prayer.")

Setting the Table

LEADER: *On this table, in the midst of this community, we place these symbols to remind us that Christ is with us and that his promises are true.*

READER 1: (lighting the candle) *A candle, to remind us to walk in the light of Christ's presence. "I am the light of the world. Whoever follows me will never walk in darkness but will have the light of life"* (John 8:12).

READER 2: (placing the basket of bread on the table) *Bread, to remind us of Christ's gifts of life and love. "I am the bread of life. . . . The bread that I will give for the life of the world is my flesh"* (John 6:48, 51).

READER 3: (placing the pitcher of water on the table) *Water, to remind us that Christ offers us living water and calls us to live life to the fullest. "I came that they may have life, and have it abundantly"* (John 10:10).

ALL: *Christ, we welcome your presence with us. May the food and companionship we share nourish our bodies, hearts, and minds. May our spirits be refreshed as we gather in your presence. Be with us now as you are with all people in all times and places. Amen.*

Serving the Meal

READER 1: *Jesus said, "The bread of God is that which comes down from heaven and gives life to the world" (John 6:33). We take this bread as a symbol of the strength that comes from God, remembering that we can do all things through Christ who strengthens us. (See Philippians 4:13.)*

[Reader 1 will take the basket of bread and, offering a word of blessing ("*Name*, the gift of life and strength"), will hold it while the person to the right takes a piece of bread and places it on his or her plate. Then, Reader 1 will pass the basket to that person, who will serve the person to his or her right in the same way. Continue around the table until everyone has a piece of bread.]

READER 2: *Jesus said, "Those who drink of the water that I will give them will never be thirsty. The water that I will give will become in them a spring of water gushing up to eternal life" (John 4:14). We receive this water as a symbol of the abundant life Christ offers us.*

[Reader 2 will take the pitcher of water and, offering words of blessing ("*Name*, the promise of abundant life"), will fill the cup of the person to the left. Then, Reader 2 will pass the pitcher to that person, who will serve the person to his or her left in the same way. Continue around the table until everyone has a cup of water.]

READER 3:

Let us pray:
God of Life and Love,
Wake us up to your presence in this moment
so that this everyday meal becomes an eternal feast,
so that our eating and drinking unites us with Christ,
so we know that you live in us and that we live in you,

so that we live in the world, knowing it is yours.
Amen.

(Reader 3 will invite the group to enjoy the meal as they share their stories of faith.)

Sharing Our Stories

LEADER: *In the past few weeks, how have you seen God working in your life? in the lives of others in our group? in the world around us? How are you experiencing connection with one another and with God?*

(Allow time for everyone to respond, if they wish. When everyone has finished the meal, you can invite the group into a time of singing.)

Closing Music

(Choose a song that celebrates communion with one another and with God, such as "This Is the Air I Breathe" or "They Will Know We Are Christians by Our Love.")

Sending Forth with Thanks

ALL: *Loving God,*
We thank you for this meal and for the friends around this table.
In the sharing of your life-giving bread and your living water,
may we come to know communion with you and one another.
Move in us so that we are awake in each moment
to experience the abundant life you offer.
Make us aware of our guilt and shame,
and compassionately transform us with grace.
Bring us to life with your Spirit,
so that we can listen deeply and offer empathy to others.
Abide in us so that we will have strength and peace
to be powerful forces of love in the world.

Allow us to arise in the grace of your love,
  fully alive to our purpose and grounded in eternal hope.
Through this shared meal with a community that is growing in love,
  help us to know our worth and to feel in our souls that we truly belong.
Thank you for your incredible invitation to experience your love and grace.
We praise you and look forward to sharing with all your people
  your promise of abundant life in Christ. Amen.

Reflection

Once the students have shared the love feast together, give them some time to reflect on the experience. Blank space is provided on page 74 of the Student Guide. You might paraphrase or read aloud the following paragraph.

> *Take a few moments to reflect on your experience of the love feast. How did you feel about participating in this agape meal immediately following your conversations about shame? What do you notice about your thoughts, emotions, and physical body after this meal? Write or draw anything that comes to mind.*

If you have time, invite students to share some of their reflections.

ARISE (5–10 MINUTES)

As you close this session, read aloud or paraphrase the sentences that follow to offer a summary of the session and a reminder to complete the daily home practices. (The instructions for home practices can be found in the Student Guide on page 75.)

> *Today, you learned about overcoming shame and experiencing connection and communion. Use the courageous conversations and loving-kindness meditation to continue overcoming shame and seeking connection to yourself, God, and others.*

Be sure to inform students of your plans for the prayer walk in Week 6. Let them know where the group will meet, what kind of clothes to wear, and any other pertinent information. (Also, be sure to let parents know if you plan to meet in a different setting next week.) Then, invite students to read the closing blessing together.

HOME PRACTICES FOR WEEK 5

1. Continue to practice loving-kindness meditation each day.

2. Have a courageous conversation about shame with a friend or family member this week. Then, reread the Abide section and record any further insights you have about the love feast.

3. Keep track of your observations in the practice journal section of the Student Guide (beginning on page 76). For example, on Day 1, enter the date you practiced and the practice: "loving-kindness meditation." Then, record anything you notice about your thoughts, emotions, and physical body. Keep in mind that there is no wrong answer.

4. Check in with your practice partner at least twice this week. Talk about the courageous conversations you had in this session and about the experience of letting go of the thoughts that lead to shame.

CLOSING BLESSING

Say the closing blessing together as you prepare to leave. (The blessing is printed in the Student Guide on page 75.)

We are awakening to abundant life.
We are becoming aware of our worth and belonging.
We are becoming alive to our senses, thoughts, and emotions.
We are abiding in the love and grace of God.
We arise now to live a life as connected, whole people.

WEEK 6

CONNECTING TO CREATION

EXPERIENCING
AWE OF
NATURE

MATERIALS

For this session, you will need the following items:

- Small sticky notes
- Markers
- Student Guides and/or journals
- Pens and pencils
- Computer and screen (optional)

LEADER PREPARATION

- **Review the full session**.
- **Locate the "Awakened Life" word wall.** If you have been building a word wall, make sure the students can access it again this week. You also may wish to provide a new color sticky note for this week.
- **Prepare for the prayer walk**. The walking meditation is intended to take place outside. You may have arranged to hold this session at a local park, nature preserve, community garden, or farm. If so, you might want to shorten the introduction materials to allow as much time as possible for walking in nature. Or you may be holding the session at your church. If so, find an appropriate place for students to walk on or near church property. If the weather does not permit you to go outside, you might create an indoor walking space that incorporates natural elements. You could collect some natural objects (stones, leaves, shells, dried flowers, etc.), create a PowerPoint of nature photographs, and/or make a playlist of nature sounds. Encourage students to be mindful of their feet touching the ground and the sensations around them, even if they are unable to be outside.
- **Make plans for the shared meal in Week 7.** Next week, you will be preparing and eating a meal together as a group. Consider how you might engage all of the students in this process. For instance, you might assign students

to bring in various ingredients. Simple ideas for collaborative meals include tacos (tortillas, lettuce, tomatoes, cheese, etc.) or pizza (crust, sauce, cheese, etc.). If you have chosen to do this week's prayer walk at a farm or community garden, you might let the students select some items there to use in next week's meal. If cooking a meal together is not possible, you might plan for a potluck or delivery option. You will want to have a plan in place before you begin this session so that you can discuss the meal with your students and make any necessary assignments. If students will be responsible for bringing an ingredient or dish, remember to communicate this information to their parents or guardians. You might also want to send reminders before the next session.

SCHEDULE FOR WEEK 6

 AWAKE (5–10 MINUTES)
CHECK-IN
INTRODUCTION

 AWARE (10–15 MINUTES)
THE WHY
JOURNAL

 ALIVE (20–25 MINUTES)
PRAYER WALK

 ABIDE (10 MINUTES)
CENTERING PRAYER

 ARISE (5–10 MINUTES)
REVIEW HOME PRACTICES
CLOSING BLESSING

AWAKE (5–10 MINUTES)

This week, you will want to shift the students' focus. For the last two weeks, they have been working to deepen their connection with others. This week, they will begin to awaken to the power of our connection with nature. After students have had the opportunity to review the home practices from the last week, mark the transition and introduce the new concept.

CHECK-IN

Before the session, place sticky notes and markers on a table. Write "Connecting to Others" on a piece of paper, and display it on or above the table as a reminder of the focus of Weeks 5 and 6.

Begin your time together by lighting a candle or saying a prayer together. Then, ask students to write on a sticky note the word or words that best sum up what they have discovered about their relationships over the past two weeks. You might invite students to share these words as they add them to the "Awakened Life" word wall. Then, invite students to review the home practices using the prompts that follow. (If you have chosen to meet in a new space for this session, you may forego the word wall and review for this week.)

- *Look over your journal reflections on the love feast. What insights did you have?*

- *What reflections did you have about practicing loving-kindness meditation? How did your experience change over the week as you continued to extend loving-kindness to someone with whom you have a difficult relationship?*

INTRODUCTION TO WEEK 6: EXPERIENCING AWE OF NATURE

You may want to introduce the new theme—Connecting to Nature—by paraphrasing or reading aloud the paragraphs that follow. (These paragraphs can also be found in the Student Guide on page 80.)

> *Do you remember the last time you sat appreciating the rustling of green leaves against an indigo sky? The sun warmed you, and the wind caressed*

your face. Maybe on another day you went outside after a rain, smelled the clean air, and counted the earthworms on the sidewalk. A puddle of water called to you to jump and splash. The wet soil tempted you to squish together a mud pie with your bare hands. What about an evening outside when you glimpsed the first star appearing at dusk, and you waited for the flash of a firefly to chase? Even better, you stayed still so the fireflies came close, and you were surrounded by their light under the glow of starlight. These moments are gifts from our Creator God.

In the beginning, God placed the earth neither too far nor too close to the sun to perfectly sustain life. Then, God created us along with plants and animals and gave us the role of gardener, steward of the planet. For some, this stewardship means digging in the earth, planting the seeds, and nurturing the growth of food and flowers. For all, it means connecting to the seasons, praying for the farmers, conserving resources, and holding awe for the cycle of life. Yet, with the convenience of grocery stores and modern transportation, we are more disconnected from how our food is raised. In our busyness, we consume the earth's resources with little appreciation. We go from our homes to our cars to our schools with our earbuds in, without noticing the sun, the trees, the clouds, or the bird's chirp of greeting. Connecting to nature is another key to wholeness.

Reflection

Ask students to turn to a person close to them and to share their response to this prompt.

- *Describe a time when you felt connected to nature or a moment in nature that woke you up to something extraordinary.*

AWARE (10–15 MINUTES)

In this section, you will provide information about the health benefits of spending time outdoors and then invite students to consider their experiences with nature.

THE WHY

You may read or paraphrase the paragraph that follows. (This paragraph can also be found in the Student Guide on page 81.)

> *Scientific research shows that time outdoors has a positive impact on our physical, emotional, mental, and spiritual health. Spending time in nature may help to address specific problems, such as depression and anxiety. Research in* Environmental Health Perspectives *tells us this: "Contact with nature offers promise both as prevention and as treatment across the life course."[1] Yet, even though we hear reports about the importance of time in nature, the time we spend outside is not increasing. Media consumption, however, is on the rise; studies indicate that teens spend an average of nine hours a day plugged in.[2] Research demonstrates that visiting parks, camping, hunting, fishing, and playing outdoors have all declined substantially over recent decades.[3]*

JOURNAL

Next, allow the students time to reflect on their connection to God through the natural world with the prompts below. Space for writing or drawing is provided in the Student Guide on pages 81–82. (If you are in a park or nature preserve for this session, you might choose instead to encourage students to respond to these prompts during the week as a part of their home practice.)

- Describe the most recent time you spent outside. Where were you? What could you see, hear, smell, taste, and touch?

- Where is your favorite place to go outside? What do you like about this place? How do you feel when you are there?

- Describe a time when you experienced a deep sense of connection with God in the natural world. How and where did you experience this connection?

- What keeps you from being outside more often? What do you think keeps other people inside?

ALIVE (20-25 MINUTES)

PRAYER WALK

In this section, you will invite students to go on a prayer walk outside. Review with them the instructions that follow. (The instructions also can be found in the Student Guide on page 83). Emphasize the importance of turning off or putting away phones and other electronic devices during the walk. "Fasting" from technology during the walk will limit distractions and allow the students to be deeply aware of God's creation. Invite them to be thankful for all that they see, hear, smell, or touch in the natural world. When students return, ask them to reflect on the experience.

Instructions

1. Set a timer for fifteen minutes on your phone, but then put it away.

2. Practice paying attention and focusing on the natural world.

3. If your mind wanders, bring yourself gently back into focus without judgment.

4. Silently express gratitude for what you see, hear, smell, and touch.

5. Pray for connection with and appreciation for the world around you.

6. Pray that all the living things you encounter will experience abundant life.

7. If the weather is nice, you might take off your shoes. Feel grounded in the earth that solidly supports you.

8. Finally, find a comfortable place. Pick one living organism you find there (for example, a leaf, a blade of grass, a bug, or tree bark). Spend your last five minutes looking at it with a loving gaze. Open yourself to what God is revealing to you through this small part of creation.

NOTE FOR LEADERS: If the weather does not permit students to go outdoors for a prayer walk, you might decorate a large indoor space with items from nature—leaves, grass, bark, moss, fragrant flowers or plants—or even photos of nature so that students can experience the prayer walk indoors.

Reflection

Invite students to share their observations from the prayer walk. If you wish, you can use these questions. (They can also be found in the Student Guide on page 84.)

- *What did you notice during your prayer walk? What stood out to you? What did you see, hear, smell, or touch?*
- *What happened in your body as you experienced the outdoors?*
- *How did you feel before you started the walk? How do you feel now?*

Conclude the reflection time by asking students to think of two or three words that come to mind when they think about their prayer walk experience. Invite students to write these words in the blank circle provided in the Student Guide on page 84. (You also might ask them to add these words to the "Awakened Life" word wall when you return from the prayer walk or during check-in at your next session.)

ABIDE (10 MINUTES)

CENTERING PRAYER

In this section, you will introduce the students to the spiritual practice of Centering Prayer. You might start by paraphrasing or reading the sentences that follow.

> *The practice of Centering Prayer is an invitation to focus on God's presence in and around you. Take some time with this practice to consider your awe of God's creation.*

Next, you will invite the students to choose a sacred word to return to when their minds begin to wander. They might use one of the words they wrote after the prayer walk. Review with the students the instructions that follow. (These instructions can also found in the Student Guide on pages 84–85.)

Instructions

1. Pick a sacred word to use during your prayer time to help you focus on God. You might use one of the words you wrote after the prayer walk. Or you might choose another sacred word, such as *Creator, awe, connected, nature,* or *beauty.*

2. Sit comfortably in silence with your eyes closed and your mind open to God.

3. When your mind begins to wander and thoughts begin to form, silently repeat your sacred word and gently return to focusing on God's presence around you and within you.

4. When the Centering Prayer time is over, before you open your eyes, take a few moments to observe any thoughts, emotions, or physical sensations you experienced during the prayer.

Allow the students to remain in prayer for three to five minutes, depending on their comfort level. When the allotted time is up, ask the students, with eyes still closed, to reflect silently on what they experienced during the prayer.

To close the prayer time, quietly say, "Amen." Invite the students to open their eyes as they are ready. Then ask them to share what they noticed about their thoughts, emotions, and bodies. Encourage them to log their reflections in Day 1 of the Daily Practice Journal beginning on page 87 in the Student Guide.

Prayer

Ask students to say this prayer together as you conclude this practice. (This prayer can be found on page 85 of the Student Guide.)

God, help me stay connected to my sense of awe for creation. Amen.

ARISE (5–10 MINUTES)

Encourage your students to continue a daily practice of Centering Prayer and to journal their reflections. You can also invite them to take a few outdoor prayers walks or short tech fasts (starting with an hour a day and building up) during the week. Before you conclude the session, spend some time describing the meal you will prepare and share together next week. If students will be bringing ingredients or dishes, you will want to make those assignments now and send reminders before the next session.

You may wish to use the sentences that follow to review the session and practices. (These can also be found in the Student Guide on page 86.)

Today, you learned about the power of connecting with nature. Use the home practices to continue increasing your awareness of the natural environment and to notice how spending time in creation affects your body, mind, and spirit.

HOME PRACTICES FOR WEEK 6

1. Practice Centering Prayer each day for at least three minutes. You can use the same sacred word you used today or choose a new word each day.

2. Keep track of your observations in the practice journal section of the Student Guide (beginning on page 87). For example, on Day 1, enter the date you practiced and the practice: "Centering Prayer." Then, record anything you notice about your thoughts, emotions, and physical body. Keep in mind that there is no wrong answer.

3. Get outside! Take a prayer walk in your neighborhood at least twice this week. If weather keeps you inside, try a tech fast. Spend at least an hour away from your phone and other screens.

4. Check in with your practice partner at least twice this week. You might want to take a silent prayer walk together and then talk about how you felt during that experience.

CLOSING BLESSING

Say the closing blessing together as you prepare to leave. (The blessing is printed in the Student Guide on page 86.)

We are awakening to abundant life.
We are becoming aware of our worth and belonging.
We are becoming alive to our senses, thoughts, and emotions.
We are abiding in the love and grace of God.
We arise now to live a life as connected, whole people.

WEEK 7

CONNECTING TO CREATION

SHARING A MEAL OF INTENTION

MATERIALS

For this session, you will need the following items:

- Small sticky notes
- Markers
- Internet access
- Student Guides and/or journals
- Pens and pencils
- Food and utensils for meal

LEADER PREPARATION

- **Review the full session**.
- **Locate the "Awakened Life" word wall.** If you have been building a word wall, make sure the students can access it. You also may wish to provide a new color sticky note for this week.
- **Make research assignments.** Students will be doing some Internet research on what it takes to grow or produce each item they will eat today. For instance, if you are planning to make or order pizza, they might research cheese, tomatoes, or flour. Think ahead about which ingredients you want them to research in small groups. If some students will not have smartphones to do the research, make accommodations in advance.
- **Arrange for the shared meal.** If you decided on pizza, make sure you place the order to arrive in time for the session. If you decided to prepare tacos in the church kitchen, make sure you have the necessary kitchen equipment ready. Consider what task each student can do to help with room setup, food prep, and cleanup. If possible, arrange the room so that everyone can eat together at one table.

SCHEDULE FOR WEEK 7

 AWAKE (5–10 MINUTES)
CHECK-IN
INTRODUCTION

 AWARE (5–10 MINUTES)
THE WHY

 ALIVE (10–15 MINUTES)
GROUP RESEARCH

 ABIDE (25–30 MINUTES)
MINDFUL EATING

 ARISE (5 MINUTES)
REVIEW HOME PRACTICES
CLOSING BLESSING

AWAKE (5–10 MINUTES)

CHECK-IN

As in previous sessions, you will begin by checking in about how the home practices and the past week went for each student. You can use the following paragraph and prompts to spark that discussion.

> *This week, we will focus on experiencing God through our connections with self, others, and nature in the sharing of a meal. But first, let's check in regarding your daily practices.*

- *How did your practices go this week? What sacred word or words did you use during Centering Prayer? What insights did you receive through this practice?*

- *Where did your prayer walks lead you? What did you notice while praying with your feet? What did this practice teach you about praying for and connecting with others?*

- *If you tried a tech fast, what did you notice about yourself during your fast? In what ways did you feel more alive when you were unplugged?*

After the discussion, pass out sticky notes and markers. Ask students to write on a sticky note one sensory observation they made during their prayer walks. If they did not have an opportunity to take a prayer walk during the week, they may add an observation they recall from the experience during the last session. You might encourage students to share the words they wrote as they add their sticky notes to the "Awakened Life" word wall.

INTRODUCTION TO WEEK 7: SHARING A MEAL OF INTENTION

Invite the students to begin thinking about their relationship with food. You may paraphrase or read aloud the introduction that follows. (This material can also be found in the Student Guide on page 92.)

> *For weeks, we have been working to quiet our minds and to limit distractions so that we are able to experience God through our connections with self, others, and nature. The meal we are going to share today brings all of our work together. Making, preparing, and sharing food provides an opportunity to experience the presence of God. Meals give us a glimpse of heaven. Creation offers us nourishment, friends bless us with their presence, we share ourselves in conversation, and God binds us all together in love.*

Pause here. Ask students to turn to the person next to them and to share with each other their response to this prompt:

- *Describe a meal you vividly remember. Who was present? What did you eat? Why do you think this meal stands out in your memory?*

The shared meal is important throughout different cultures. The Lakota Sioux people have a prayer, "Mitakuye Oyasin," that celebrates God's creation through our connection to minerals, plants, animals, humans, and Spirit. Our indigenous brothers and sisters remind us that when the earth thrives, we thrive, and that when the earth hurts, so do we.

> **You are all my relations, my relatives, without whom I would not live.**
> **LAKOTA SIOUX PRAYER**

Meals are experiences of radical hospitality and love in the Judeo-Christian faith tradition. At a meal, care is extended for all who join around the table. Jesus invited himself to a greedy tax collector's house and restored that man to his community. (See Luke 19:1–10.) At a prestigious dinner party, Jesus allowed a "sinful woman" to anoint his feet with oil and then blessed her with healing and hope. (See Luke 7:36-37.) Another time, when thousands were gathered for his teachings, the disciples wanted Jesus to send the people away to feed themselves at mealtime. Yet, Jesus invited a miraculous sharing, and all were fed to the point of full bellies and souls. (See Mark 6:30-44.) Powerful things happen at meals. Lives are shared and connected by the simple yet profound act of breaking bread together as we open ourselves to God's possibilities for our lives.

AWARE (5-10 MINUTES)

In this section, you will introduce the students to research about the ways our fast-food culture has disconnected us from our food and about the health benefits of shared meals.

THE WHY

Before you provide this information, you might ask for a show of hands to see how many students eat while using their phones. Invite students to reflect on the differences between meals they have eaten with and without their phones. Then, paraphrase or read aloud the paragraph that follows. (This material can also be found in the Student Guide on page 93.)

In our fast-food culture, the preparing and sharing of meals often goes missing. A 2018 survey revealed that almost one in three Americans "can't get through a meal without being on their phones."[1] Over 70 percent of the two thousand people surveyed reported that they often watch TV while eating.[2] These habits lead to disconnection from the people with whom we are eating as well as disconnection from our food. While distracted by their phones, people are more likely to chew less and to eat more. Eating on the go rather than around a table distances us from the fellowship involved in preparing and eating a meal. It also decreases our knowledge of and gratitude for the efforts of all who made that meal possible. To get the physical, emotional, and spiritual health benefits of shared meals, three things are crucial: putting down your phone, engaging in conversation, and being grateful for the meal in front of you.

ALIVE (10-15 MINUTES)

After sharing "The Why" information and statistics, invite the students to do some Internet research about the food they will be eating.

GROUP RESEARCH

Ask the students to form small groups of two or three people. Based on the meal the students will eat together, assign each small group an ingredient to research. For example, if you are having pizza, ask each group to research one of the ingredients—flour, tomatoes, cheese, or garlic—and its pathway to your table. You can use the paragraph that follows to introduce the research project to your students. (This material can also be found on page 94 of the Student Guide.)

> To truly be grateful for the meal you are about to share, consider its origins. Take some time to think about the people involved and processes required to grow, produce, and transport the various ingredients for this meal. Be grateful for those who helped to get this food to you, and be aware of how your food's production affects the earth.

Before the students begin to work in their groups, consider walking them through an example. For instance, you might ask the students to brainstorm a list of all the people connected to the tomatoes you will use for your meal. This list might include farmers to grow and harvest the tomatoes, a driver to transport the tomatoes from the farm to the store, grocery store clerks to stock the produce, and so on. Then, work together to explore the positive and negative effects for each person involved and for the earth.

Instructions

Once the students understand the assignment, invite them to use their phones to find out as much as they can about the dinner ingredient assigned to their group. (If some students do not have phones, you can provide them with computer access. Or you might invite groups to jot down a list of what they know and what they wonder about the production of the designated food item.) Ask students to record what they learn about how this ingredient was likely grown or made. Also, encourage them to note any social justice issues related to the production or shipping of this item and any nutritional information about the ingredient that might be relevant. Let the students know that they will find questions to direct their research on page 94 of the Student Guide. (These questions are also printed below.)

1. Where was this ingredient likely grown? Is it in season in our region right now?

2. What went into the growing and/or making of this ingredient?

3. What people may have been involved in growing or making this ingredient and in getting it to our table? Were any of these people working under oppressive conditions?

4. How was the earth positively and negatively affected by the growth or production of this ingredient? How eco-friendly were the processes or chemicals involved in providing us with this part of our meal?

5. What nutritional value does this ingredient offer our bodies? Why is that information relevant to an awakened life?

6. What unanswered questions do you have?

Discussion

After allowing five or ten minutes for research, bring the students together. Allow each group to report on what they have learned or the questions they still have. Conclude this section by asking the following question:

- *What did you learn that makes you especially thankful for the food we are about to eat?*

ABIDE (25–30 MINUTES)

MINDFUL EATING: SHARING A MEAL OF INTENTION

This week's practice is mindful eating, or sharing a meal of intention. In this section, you may want to spend ten minutes guiding the students through the meal preparation (unless you ordered delivery), five to ten minutes eating in silence, and another five to ten minutes engaging in a group conversation about the process. Feel free to modify this schedule as needed to accommodate the meal plans you have made for your group.

If you have access to a church kitchen, then you may decide to prepare the meal together. Assign different food prep chores, and invite students to pay attention to the physical processes of washing, chopping, and cooking. Encourage them to be aware of the sensory components—the sound of the knife hitting the cutting board, the smell of the sliced onion, and the smooth texture of the tomato.

Mindful Eating Meditation

Once the meal is ready and everyone is seated, ask students, if they haven't already, to silence their phones. Offer a blessing of gratitude for the meal and for the opportunity to share a meal together in a new way. Then, use the steps that follow to guide students through a mindful eating meditation. Once you have led them through the first bite, we recommend that you ask everyone at the table to spend the first five or ten minutes of the meal in silence to focus on the sensations associated with eating.

- **Holding**: *First, take a piece of food from your plate. Hold it with a utensil or in the palm of your hand.*

- **Seeing**: *Take time to look closely at it; focus on the food with intention, and gaze at it with care and full attention. Imagine that you have never seen food like this. Let your eyes explore every part of it.*

- **Touching**: *Run your fingers over the piece of food, and explore its texture. You might close your eyes if that enhances your sense of touch.*

- **Smelling**: *Hold the food beneath your nose. With each inhalation, take in any smell, aroma, or fragrance that may arise. As you do this, notice anything interesting that may be happening in your mouth or stomach.*

- **Placing**: *Now, slowly bring the food up to your lips. Gently place it in your mouth. Without chewing, spend a few moments focusing on the sensations of having it in your mouth.*

- **Tasting**: *When you are ready, prepare to chew. Very consciously, take one or two bites into the food, and notice what happens. Then, continue chewing and experience any waves of taste. Without swallowing yet, notice the sensations of taste and texture in your mouth.*

- **Swallowing**: *When you feel ready to swallow the food, see if you can first detect the intention to swallow as it comes to you so that even this often-unnoticed sensation is experienced consciously before you swallow.*

- **Following**: *Finally, see if you can feel what is left of the food moving down into your stomach. Sense how your body is feeling after you have completed this exercise.*[3]

Instructions for Sharing a Meal of Intention

After the students have experienced the first bite of their meal as a guided meditation, encourage them to use a similarly mindful approach to the entire meal. Explain that for each of you to be fully present to your senses and to the beauty of the food you will be eating, you will spend the first five to ten minutes of this meal in silence. Before the silence begins, you might review the food mindfulness instructions that follow. (These instructions are also in the Student Guide on page 95.)

- *Put away all screens so you can be fully present during the meal.*
- *Practice being silent for the first five or ten minutes of the meal.*
- *Consider what you smell, feel, taste, and experience with each bite.*
- *Try to chew each bite thirty times.*
- *Think back to your research. What people were involved and what processes went into the making of this food?*
- *Take a moment to be thankful for each step of this process and all the people and natural resources needed to nourish your body in this moment.*

Begin the time of silence, and let the meal continue. After five or ten minutes of silence, invite students into a group conversation about the experience.

Meal Conversation Starters

Students may continue eating while they talk. If you have a small group, you might choose to ask some questions from the list of conversation starters that follows. If you have a large group, you might encourage students to use these questions to spark conversation in smaller groups around the table. (The conversation starters can be found in the Student Guide on pages 95–96.)

- *How did you feel while eating in silence without your phone and intentionally staying present to your eating experience?*
- *How did your research about the ingredients and the people who grew and prepared them affect your eating experience?*
- *How did this meal compare to other meals you eat at home or at school?*
- *What are your meal practices at home? Does your family eat together, or does everyone eat separately?*
- *What kind of conversations do you have during meals at school?*
- *What practices could you incorporate into your life to show gratitude for the food you eat?*

ARISE (5 MINUTES)

While the group is still seated at the table, review the session using the sentences that follow. (This material is also printed in the Student Guide on page 97.)

> *Today, you awakened to experiencing God through your connections with self, others, and creation in the sharing of a meal. Use the home practices to help you stay awake to this interconnectedness.*

Remind students of the home practices for the coming week, and encourage them to record their reflections on the meal you shared together as the Day 1 entry on page 98 in the Student Guide. Also, since next week will be your last session, you may want to prepare the students for the end of their time together and invite them to talk about any feelings they might be experiencing as the study draws to a close. Then, ask the students to say the closing blessing as you end your meal and your time together in this session.

HOME PRACTICES FOR WEEK 7

1. Practice mindful eating during one meal each day. Try adding more meals so that mindful eating gradually becomes a regular practice.

2. Keep track of your observations in the practice journal section of the Student Guide (beginning on page 98). For example, on Day 1, enter the date you practiced and the practice: "mindful eating." Then, record your thoughts, emotions, and any physical sensations you notice. Keep in mind that there is no wrong answer.

3. Check in with your practice partner at least twice this week. Share a meal together if you can.

CLOSING BLESSING

Say the closing blessing together as you prepare to leave. (The blessing is printed in the Student Guide on page 97.)

We are awakening to abundant life.
We are becoming aware of our worth and belonging.
We are becoming alive to our senses, thoughts, and emotions.
We are abiding in the love and grace of God.
We arise now to live a life as connected, whole people.

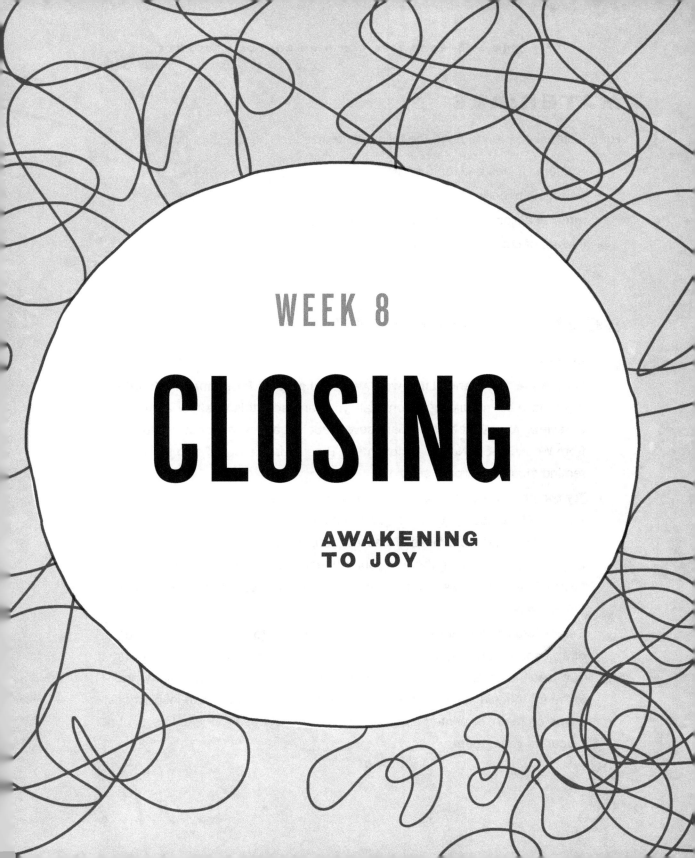

WEEK 8

CLOSING

AWAKENING TO JOY

MATERIALS

For this session, you will need the following items:

- Student Guides and/or journals
- Pens and pencils
- Internet access, computer, and speakers (optional)
- Tokens of course completion (optional)

LEADER PREPARATION

- **Review the full session**.
- **Locate the "Awakened Life" word wall, and prepare for a time of reflection.** If you have been building a word wall, you can use it this week for a time of review. You might also prepare seven labels, each with a session title from Weeks 2–8 ("Noticing Thoughts," "Present in the Body," and so on), to remind students of past sessions.
- **Try the practices.** The Awake section incorporates a gratitude meditation; and the Abide section offers a new spiritual practice, the Daily Examen. Especially if these practices are new to you, we encourage you to try them before presenting them to your students. The audio track for the "Week 8: Gratitude Meditation" can be found at UpperRoomBooks.com/ TheAwakenedLife.
- **Select tokens to honor course completion**. Often, to symbolize the ending of an important event, a small token is given to each participant. The giving of a token is completely optional but might be meaningful to your students. Ideas for this gift include notebooks, journals, small stones with inspirational words on them, or printed photos of the group. Feel free to make this symbol unique to your group.

SCHEDULE FOR WEEK 8

 AWAKE (10–15 MINUTES)
CHECK-IN
INTRODUCTION
GRATITUDE MEDITATION

 AWARE (5–10 MINUTES)
GROUP REFLECTION

 ALIVE (15–20 MINUTES)
GROUP GRATITUDE EXERCISE
JOURNAL

 ABIDE (10–15 MINUTES)
DAILY EXAMEN

 ARISE (5–10 MINUTES)
REVIEW HOME PRACTICES
CLOSING BLESSING

AWAKE (10–15 MINUTES)

CHECK-IN

Once again, check in with students about their home practices. Remind students that even though the study is ending, they can carry these practices with them forever. Use the paragraph and prompts that follow to initiate this conversation.

> *Welcome to our final session together. Today, we will talk about how an awakened life is a joyful, grateful life. Let's start by checking in one last time regarding our weekly practices.*

- *How did you incorporate mindful eating into your week?*
- *Did you learn anything new about yourself? about God?*

INTRODUCTION TO WEEK 8: AWAKENING TO JOY

After you spend some time discussing the home practices, read or paraphrase the paragraph that follows to review the work the students have done so far. (This paragraph can also be found in the Student Guide on page 102.)

> *Our work together over these eight weeks is just the beginning of an awakened, abundant life. You are building the skills you need to be fully awake to your feelings and thoughts and to the ways they live in your body. This self-awareness will help you face criticism and disappointment with a sense of your own worth. This sense of worthiness will help you to build a life of connection, and these connections will strengthen you to face challenges. In the Christian tradition, connection to the Spirit of God allows for a life of "love, joy, peace, patience, kindness, goodness, faithfulness, gentleness, and self-control" (Gal. 5:22-23, CEB). A life that cultivates these qualities can persevere through struggles.*

GRATITUDE MEDITATION

The best way to set the stage for the last session is to introduce the gratitude meditation and then try the practice together. You may want to read aloud the sentences that follow.

> *One way we can begin to awaken to joy is to practice gratitude. Often, we forget—or simply take for granted—all the things in our lives that are cause for thankfulness. Being aware of these things takes some practice.*

Listen > *Week 8: Gratitude Meditation*

To guide the group through the gratitude meditation, you may play the audio track ("Week 8: Gratitude Meditation") that can be accessed at UpperRoomBooks.com/TheAwakenedLife.

Or you can read the script that follows, reading slowly and giving students space to pause and to notice their breath and thoughts.

Begin by finding a quiet place where you can be still. Sit upright in a comfortable, supported position, where your back and neck are straight but relaxed. If you feel comfortable, allow your eyes to gently close, or simply gaze at a spot in front of you. Take a slow, deep breath to bring yourself into the present moment. As you bring your awareness to your breath, notice the inhalations and exhalations. Then, take a few moments to scan your body, noticing any areas of tension or stress and allowing those muscles to relax.

Now that your body, thoughts, and emotions are a bit more centered, begin to focus your awareness on the events, experiences, people, places, pets, or possessions for which you feel grateful. First, you might recall that you already have several marvelous gifts available to you in this moment. Regardless of your circumstances, you are sharing in the gift of life right now. Take a moment to be grateful for your heartbeat. Notice how your heart feels beating in your chest, and take a moment to express thanks for the work that your heart does to pump life-giving blood throughout your body. Then, extend this awareness with gratitude for your senses. Notice what you hear or smell or feel in the room, and be grateful for the gift of your senses.

Now, take a moment to note all the things that make your life easier and more comfortable. Maybe express gratitude for electricity, the ability to drive a car, the access to information that technology offers, the clean water that flows from your tap, the roof over your head. Then, take a moment to thank all the people who have worked hard, many without knowing it, to make your life full. Thank the farmers who grow your food, the postal workers who deliver your mail, the technicians who work to maintain your Internet services, and the teams who build the roads and highways. Consider the people and pets in your personal sphere of influence, and extend thanks to each of the individuals who bring joy to your life.

Gradually bring your awareness back to your breath. Notice if it has shifted or changed at all during this meditation. Notice how your body is feeling at this moment.

As you are ready, open your eyes.

Prayer

As the meditation ends, ask students to say this prayer with you. (It is printed on page 102 of the Student Guide.)

> **God, help me continue to be awake to your presence in all aspects of my life. Amen.**

Reflection

Invite the group to talk about their experience of the gratitude meditation by responding to these prompts:

- *How did you feel as you participated in the gratitude meditation?*
- *Think back to the first time you practiced meditation in Week 1 (awareness meditation). How was your experience today similar? How was it different?*

AWARE (5-10 MINUTES)

In this section, you will invite students to reflect on the past seven weeks by reexamining the word wall they have created.

GROUP REFLECTION

To segue into a time of reflection, you might paraphrase or read aloud the paragraph that follows. (This material can be found on page 103 of the Student Guide.)

Spiritual disciplines and mindfulness can help to reduce stress. All the mindful, meditative, and spiritual practices you have experienced during our time together help to train your mind to tolerate negativity, boredom, and anxiety. These practices offer calm in the storms of life by connecting you to God through your relationships with self, others, and nature. Today, let's use this time to stay awake and aware of what you have learned during our time together.

If you created labels with the session titles, place them around the "Awakened Life" word wall. Invite students to take a few moments to look at the word wall they have created. You can use the questions that follow to guide the group in a time of reflection.

- *As you look at our word wall, what words or phrases stand out to you today?*

    To prompt discussion, consider asking each student to name a word or phrase.

- *Remembering each session, think about what was most meaningful to you. What words would you like to add to our word wall?*

    You may want to read each session title one at a time and give students a few minutes to reflect in silence before they respond.

- *After all these weeks, what does "awakened life" mean to you now?*

ALIVE (15-20 MINUTES)

During this final Alive section, you will invite students to practice gratitude for one another and for the group. Then, give them time to write about insights they have gained and ways they have grown over the course of the previous seven weeks.

GROUP GRATITUDE EXERCISE

The group gratitude exercise can be an opportunity to reflect on the connections made between group members and to express the value of each person in the group. To introduce the exercise, read the sentences that follow.

> *Joy is discovered through gratitude. One great source of joy is the time we have had together as a group. Communicating these feelings of gratitude is a powerful way to express appreciation and love for one another. To celebrate our time together, we are going to form gratitude circles.*

Invite students to form two groups with an equal number of people. (You may want to join one of the groups, especially if another person is needed to achieve an even number.) Ask one group to form a circle with group members facing outward. Ask the other group to form a circle around the first one, with group members facing inward so that each person is standing across from someone in the first circle—their new partner. Next, invite the students in each pair to take turns sharing what they are grateful for about their partner and/or how their partner has helped or inspired them over the previous seven weeks. Allow a maximum of two minutes for conversation; then ask the outer circle to move clockwise while the inner circle remains stationary in order to form new pairs. Continue in this way until students are back with their original partners.

Depending on the size of your group, this exercise may take some time. If your group has more than ten students, you might want to form two or more sets of circles. Or you might allow students to walk around the room, partner up to exchange expressions of gratitude, and then find a new partner—sharing in this way with as many people as they can within the allotted time.

JOURNAL

Invite your students to consider what they want to take with them from this study. Encourage them to spend five or ten minutes jotting down some notes in response to the prompts that follow. (These prompts are also provided in the Student Guide on pages 104–105.)

- What are some things people said to you during the group gratitude exercise that you would like to remember? What about those comments was meaningful or challenged you to grow?

- What insights have you discovered about yourself during these eight weeks? In what ways have you changed? Complete this sentence: "Seven weeks ago, I was _____. Now I am _____."

- What aspect of this study are you most thankful for? What else in your life are you thankful for? How will you express your gratitude?

- Which practices do you plan to continue after this session? Why have you chosen these practices? How are they helpful to you?

ABIDE (10–15 MINUTES)

DAILY EXAMEN

As your final practice together, you will walk students through a traditional spiritual practice—the Daily Examen. You may use the sentences that follow to introduce this practice.

> *Ignatius of Loyola, a Christian leader of the sixteenth century, created the Daily Examen. An awareness and gratitude prayer, the Daily Examen can be used to reflect on your day. This practice has been passed down through generations as a way to give God our attention, to listen for God's direction, and to be thankful for all the moments in our lives.*

Instructions

Use these instructions to walk your students through the steps of the Daily Examen, pausing after each one to allow time for students to reflect. (Invite students to turn to these instructions on pages 106–107 of the Student Guide.) First, read or paraphrase the paragraph that follows.

> *In a moment, I will lead you through some simple guidelines for using the Daily Examen to reflect prayerfully on your day. When you finish reflecting on the questions in the last step, "Look Forward," please turn quietly to page 107 of your Student Guide and record any thoughts, feelings, moments of gratitude, or clarity from God about your life that you experienced during this practice. For now, close your eyes, and take a moment to focus on your breathing. Then, listen as I guide you through the steps of the Daily Examen.*[1]

1. **Invite God's Presence**: Take a few moments to invite the Holy Spirit to help you see how God was active and working in and through you during the day.

2. **Practice Gratitude**: As you replay your day in your mind, what moments are you particularly thankful for and why?

3. **Consider Your Emotions**: What emotions did you experience today? What can they teach you about yourself?

4. **Pick a Moment**: Choose a scene from your day, and pray about it with extra focus. Was there a moment in which you regretted your words, actions, or thoughts? Do you need to extend compassion to yourself or to someone else? Was there a moment that was life-giving? What does that reveal about what is truly important to you?

5. **Look Forward**: What is coming up in your life? In what areas of your life do you want to ask God for strength, direction, connection, or hope?

After the students have taken some time to record their reflections, invite them to share how they experienced the practice. Also, encourage the students to continue practicing the Daily Examen beyond this study, either on their own or with their practice partners. Let them know that as they practice, they may choose to walk through all of the steps they learned today or to focus more intentionally on a few of the steps.

ARISE (5-10 MINUTES)

As you prepare to close your final session, remind students of the importance of daily practice, even after the study is over. Consider reading or paraphrasing the sentences that follow.

> *Today is the last day of this study but only the beginning of an awakened life. I hope you carry all the practices with you and use them often so that they can support you when the struggles of life come. These mindfulness and spiritual practices will help you deepen your connection to yourself, to others, to God, and to all of creation. Being able to draw upon these practices, in good times and bad, will enable you to experience profound peace and joy.*

HOME PRACTICES FOR WEEK 8 AND BEYOND

1. Practice being awake every day through the mindfulness and spiritual exercises you have learned in this group. These exercises will keep you connected to God, yourself, others, and nature.

2. Select a sketchpad or notebook to use as a daily practice journal, and continue to draw or write about the ways your practice affects your body, mind, and spirit. Wholeness is at your fingertips.

3. Treat yourself gently with self-compassion, and give thanks for God's many blessings.

4. Stay in communication with your practice partner and with others in the group.

PRESENT TOKENS OF COMPLETION

As you close, recognize that endings can bring up all kinds of emotions. Allow students to be present with whatever they may be feeling—accomplishment, gratitude, sadness, or even relief. If you have chosen to give tokens to the students to symbolize the importance and the completion of your time together, give them out now and explain the significance of these items.

CLOSING BLESSING

Invite the students to recite the closing blessing with you.

> *We are awakening to abundant life.*
> *We are becoming aware of our worth and belonging.*
> *We are becoming alive to our senses, thoughts, and emotions.*
> *We are abiding in the love and grace of God.*
> *We arise now to live a life as connected, whole people.*

Close with these words: *May you carry this blessing with you into your awakened life.*

NOTES

Getting Started

1. Amy G. Oden, *Right Here Right Now: The Practice of Christian Mindfulness* (Nashville, TN: Abingdon Press, 2011).
2. You can learn more about trauma-informed care at http://socialwork.buffalo.edu/social -research/institutes-centers/institute-on-trauma-and-trauma-informed-care/what-is-trauma -informed-care.html.

Week 1—Introduction to the Awakened Life

1. "Adolescent Mental Health Basics," U.S. Department of Health and Human Services, February 25, 2019, https://www.hhs.gov/ash/oah/adolescent-development/mental-health/adolescent -mental-health-basics/index.html.
2. "Stress Management and Teens," American Academy of Child and Adolescent Psychiatry, January 2019, https://www.aacap.org/AACAP/Families_and_Youth/Facts_for_Families/FFF-Guide/Helping -Teenagers-With-Stress-066.aspx.
3. Hafiz and Daniel Ladinsky, "Awake Awhile," *I Heard GOD Laughing: Poems of Hope and Joy, Renderings of Hafiz by Daniel Ladinsky* (New York: Penguin, 2006), 38.
4. John O'Donohue, "The Question Holds the Lantern," *The Sun*, November 2009, http://www.the sunmagazine.org/issues/407/the-question-holds-the-lantern.

Week 2—Connecting to Self: Noticing Thoughts

1. Kristin Neff, *Self-Compassion: The Proven Power of Being Kind to Yourself* (New York: Harper Collins, 2011), 39–106.
2. Steve Bradt, "Wandering Mind Not a Happy Mind," *The Harvard Gazette*, November 11, 2010, https://news.harvard.edu/gazette/story/2010/11/wandering-mind-not-a-happy-mind/.
3. Adapted from Bob Stahl and Elisha Goldstein, *A Mindfulness-Based Stress Reduction Workbook* (Oakland, CA: New Harbinger Publications, 2010), 55–56. Stahl and Goldstein's list of negative thought patterns includes catastrophizing, mind-reading, the "shoulds," and blaming, among others.
4. Kristin Neff, quoted in Kristin Wong, "Why Self-Compassion Beats Self-Confidence," *The New York Times*, December 28, 2017, https://www.nytimes.com/2017/12/28/smarter-living/why -self-compassion-beats-self-confidence.html.
5. Neff, quoted in Wong, "Why Self-Compassion Beats Self-Confidence."

Week 3—Connecting to Self: Being Present in the Body

1. Deborah J. Cohan, "Cell Phones and College Students," *Psychology Today*, April 30, 2016, https:// www.psychologytoday.com/us/blog/social-lights/201604/cell-phones-and-college-students.

Week 4—Connecting to Others: Working Through Loneliness

1. Claudia Hammond, "The Surprising Truth about Loneliness," *BBC Future*, September 30, 2018, https://www.bbc.com/future/article/20180928-the-surprising-truth-about-loneliness.
2. Arash Emamzadeh, "Loneliness and Media Usage: A Study of 8 Million Americans," *Psychology Today*, August 22, 2019, https://www.psychologytoday.com/us/blog/finding-new-home/201908/loneliness-and-media-usage-study-8-million-americans.
3. Anna Haensch, "When Choirs Sing, Many Hearts Beat as One," NPR, July 10, 2013, https://www.npr.org/sections/health-shots/2013/07/09/200390454/when-choirs-sing-many-hearts-beat-as-one.
4. Guidelines for speakers and listeners are adapted from Parker Palmer's Circle of Trust Touchstones. These Touchstones can be found online at www.couragerenewal.org/touchstones or in Palmer, *A Hidden Wholeness: The Journey Toward an Undivided Life* (San Francisco: Jossey-Bass, 2004), 217–18.

Week 5—Connecting to Others: Working Through Shame

1. Brené Brown, *Daring Greatly: How the Courage to Be Vulnerable Transforms the Way We Live, Love, Parent, and Lead* (New York: Penguin, 2012), 71.
2. Brown, "Listening to Shame," filmed March 2012, TED video, 20:23, https://www.ted.com/talks/brene_brown_listening_to_shame.

Week 6—Connecting to Creation: Experiencing Awe of Nature

1. Howard Frumkin et al., "Nature Contact and Human Health: A Research Agenda," *Environmental Health Perspectives* 125, no. 7 (July 2017), https://ehp.niehs.nih.gov/doi/10.1289/EHP1663.
2. Hayley Tsukayama, "Teens Spend Nearly Nine Hours Every Day Consuming Media," *The Washington Post*, November 2, 2015, https://www.washingtonpost.com/news/the-switch/wp/2015/11/03/teens-spend-nearly-nine-hours-every-day-consuming-media/.
3. Frumkin et al., "Nature Contact and Human Health."

Week 7—Connecting to Creation: Sharing a Meal of Intention

1. Lily Rose, "1 in 3 Americans Can't Eat a Meal Without Being on Their Phone," *Orlando Sentinel*, January 24, 2018, http://www.orlandosentinel.com/features/food/sns-dailymeal-1867994-eat-americans-cant-eat-without-being-on-their-phones-20180124-story.html.
2. Rose, "1 in 3 Americans."
3. Adapted from Mark Williams and Danny Penman, *Mindfulness: An Eight-Week Plan for Finding Peace in a Frantic World* (New York: Rodale Books, 2012), 73–75.

Week 8—Closing: Awakening to Joy

1. Adapted from "How Can I Pray?" Loyola Press, IgnatianSpirituality.com, accessed January 14, 2019, https://www.ignatianspirituality.com/ignatian-prayer/the-examen/how-can-i-pray.

CPSIA information can be obtained
at www.ICGtesting.com
Printed in the USA
LVHW100713030720
659548LV00006B/140